ISBN 9780645591422

1st edition 2020

2nd edition 2023

Copyright © Diving Bell Education 2023

ISBN: 978-0-6455914-2-2

Diving Bell Education owns copyright of this publication. A reasonable portion of this publication (deemed up to 10%, or one chapter) may be reproduced for personal use only. The content may not otherwise be reproduced and must not be distributed or transmitted to any other person or used in any other way without the express approval of Diving Bell Education.

ISBN 9780645591422

Contents

Acknowledgement 6
The Syllabus 1
   What is the topic's focus? 1
Chapter 1: The historical habit 2
   Herodotus 4
   Thucydidean Responses 6
   CONCEPT FOCUS 1: HISTORICAL CONSCIOUSNESS 6
   Polybius and Livy 10
   Reading task 1 15
   Chapter revision statement 17
Chapter 2: Post-Classical history 18
   CONCEPT FOCUS 2: GRAND NARRATIVES 21
   History in the Middle Ages 21
   Jewish and Islamic Historians 26
   Reading task 2 29
   Chapter revision statement 32
Chapter 3: Renaissance and Reformation 33
   Recovery of Written Texts 33
   Other Peoples, Other Histories 37
   Ancients vs Moderns 39
   The Print Revolution 40
   The relegation of memory 42
   CONCEPT FOCUS 3: AUXILIARY SCIENCES 45
   History as cycles 48
   Reading task 3 50
   Chapter revision statement 53
Chapter 4: Enlightenment? 54
   The (financial) power of a good historical narrative 55

ISBN 9780645591422

CONCEPT FOCUS 4: STYLE 59
Universal progress or different standards? 59
Romanticism and German *Volkische Geschefte* 62
Reading task 4 67
Chapter revision statement 69

Chapter 5: The Academy and History 70
Historical fiction as the progenitor of 'Historism' 71
CONCEPT FOCUS 5: NATIONALIST HISTORY 85
Historism 74
Colossus: Leopold von Ranke 75
Responses and Reactions to Rankean Historicism 78
Reading task 5 88
Chapter revision statement 91

Chapter 6: The beginning of disillusionment 92
More revolutionary history 94
The Annales School 96
CONCEPT FOCUS 6: DEBATE 99
English-language social historians 101
Reading task 6 104
Chapter revision statement 106

Chapter 7: Wars in the Academy 107
The History of Women and Women in History 111
Paradigm shifts 114
CONCEPT FOCUS 7: THE HISTORIAN THEMSELVES 111
The Cultural and Linguistic Turns 116
Reading task 7 122
Chapter revision statement 125

Chapter 8: Recent times 1 – history or histories? 126
Post-Colonial Perspectives 126
History and individuals' memory 128
National and collective memory 131

History and the Culture Wars	134
Popular History	137
CONCEPT FOCUS 8: THE PUBLIC	131
Film and History	139
Reading task 8	143
Chapter revision statement	146

Chapter 9: Recent times 2 – what will be left? 147

Micro-History	147
History at the Turn of the Third Millennium	149
Professional Standards and Professional Disputes	151
CONTENT FOCUS 9: TIME	157
History in the Digital Age	153
History in the Anthropocene	157
Reading task 9	164
Chapter revision statement	167

Chapter 10: The Student Historiographer 168

The Section I Essay	168
An example	169
The historical investigation	173
An example	174
Preparing your investigation	176
Chapter revision statement	177

ISBN 9780645591422

Acknowledgement

This workbook is greatly indebted to Jeremy Popkin's *From Herodotus to H-Net*, which is one of the most widely-available, readable, and current surveys of the historiographical field. Almost all the writers, schools, and movements mentioned in this workbook are described in greater depth by Popkin, and his final chapter is useful for high-school and undergraduate students considering a career in the historical profession.

Popkin, Jeremy D. *From Herodotus to H-Net: The Story of Historiography*. Oxford University Press. Oxford: 2016.

Front cover

The image on the front cover shows American Civil War general Ulysses S. Grant supposedly in front of the Union Army headquarters at City Point, Virginia. The image, however, is a composite of the three smaller images: an informal portrait of Grant, Union Army General Alexander McDowell McCook on horseback, and an internment camp for Confederate soldiers. The composite was created by Levin Corbin Handy in 1902, from an inherited stock of Civil War negatives, which provided him with an income by satisfying what the Metropolitan Museum calls 'the steady demand for heroic images of the war, he also invented new pictures that casually blurred the line between historical fact and fiction.' It is an excellent example of historical narrative's constructed nature and the reasons behind it.

ISBN 9780645591422

The Syllabus

What is the topic's focus?

The first topic in History Extension deals with something you should already recognize: *History-writing is affected by the views, contexts, and personalities of the people who write it.*

There is no single correct way to create a written record of past events, and the varieties of historical narrative add up to very different ways of seeing and communicating the human experience.

There are also many ways to approach this topic, but this workbook will help you to develop answers to the following questions:

1. When and where do historians come from?
2. How do these contextual factors affect what historians do?
3. What are the purposes of history?
4. What do historians think they're doing when they 'do' history?
5. What tools and forms do historians use to produce history?
6. How do historians communicate among themselves?
7. Is history of any use to non-historians?
8. Who consumes the historian's product?
9. Is there any point to the discipline of History in the future?
10. What shape could it take?

It's important to be absolutely clear about the focus of this course, and how it differs from the material and approach of other history courses.

Write a sentence explaining the difference between the past, History, and historiography.

_____

_____

_____

_____

Notes

_____

_____

_____

_____

_____

_____

_____

Chapter 1: The historical habit

One of the Blau Monuments, perhaps a Sumerian boundary marker, which combines proto-cuneiform characters and illustrations from around 3100-2700 BC.

Early civilisations recorded historical information: ancient Egyptians compiled king lists, and inscriptions accompanied by sculpted battle scenes survive from Mesopotamia. Homer's *Iliad* and *Odyssey* tell the story of the Trojan War - or at least Homer's thoughts about some aspects of it. The Hebrews preserved oral stories of their origins and the deeds of their rulers, and these stories were eventually written down. In China, Confucius insisted on the importance of remembering past events (which may be told by figures such as the *pingshu* or *pinghua,* below) as a guide for appropriate conduct in the present.

Shang Tiangfang (1934–2018) was a celebrated pingshu performer, whose career coincided with the golden age of radio.

But the twentieth-century historian and philosopher of history R.G. Collingwood argued that these compositions couldn't be considered 'history' because they lacked four essential characteristics: the narration and discovery of unknown things; the focus on human actions (as opposed to divine ones); the use of an inquiry procedure, and the presence of a purpose behind the investigation.

1. What biases are revealed by Collingwood's criteria?

___

___

___

___

___

Just because priests wrote king-lists or records of deeds does not make these compositions historical, Collingwood said. They don't attempt to answer a question, they concern or refer to divine things as much as human, they lack interpretation of the evidence, and they don't add to our knowledge and understanding of ourselves as humans. Collingwood also points out that for much of Greek history, the prevailing view was that knowledge should be permanent and determinate – knowledge involved boiling data down to laws, in other words, rather than observations and speculations. But this isn't how humans act; we are changeful and frequently contradictory. Therefore, the study of human actions in the past seemed not to produce 'knowledge', as the Greeks thought of it. This gradually changed, as people (called the *logographers*) began to keep a record of what happened in their own local area, until a great clash of two large areas produced searching questions about the events and people involved.

Thus, the birth of History as a written practice began with the appearance of the first books. As the American Historical Association's website (https://www.historians.org/) says, 'History consists of making arguments about what happened in the past on the basis of what people recorded (in written documents, cultural artifacts, or oral traditions) at the time.' Only when writing becomes integral to people's engagement with life can we talk about history as a representation of what happened in the past. It's a central contention of historiography that this written representation is fundamentally different from oral stories. If you compare how you listen to a storyteller like a *pingshu* or *griot* with the way you take in the same information in a book, you'll see that written history is different – both in the way it's composed, and the way it's read.

Similarly, although many historians had written about their method and view of history, historiography as a separate discipline only really emerges at the end of the nineteenth century. By then, the intellectual 'habit' of history had been around for 2400 years and was recognised as a discrete intellectual and cultural activity susceptible to academic research.

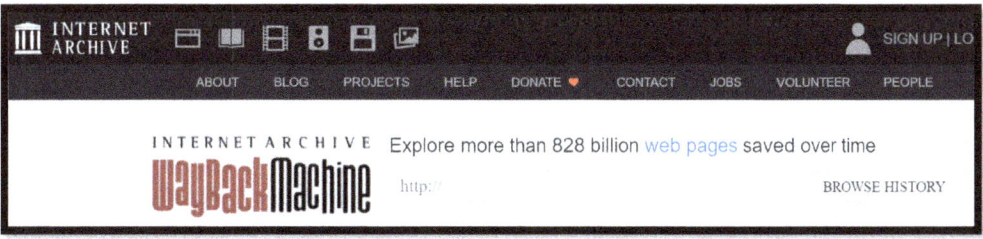

More than 800 billion web pages have been saved in the Wayback Machine. But at what point does an accretion of records become a history?

Herodotus

Timelines of history-writing give a privileged position to the fifth-century B.C. writers Herodotus and Thucydides, who embody the first sustained written interest in how and why we should preserve the past. Both men represent the broader attempt by fifth-century Greece (particularly Athens) to understand and represent accurately the contemporary world for future generations. At around the same time Socrates and Plato were enquiring into the nature of knowledge, and the playwrights Aeschylus, Sophocles and Euripides attempting psychological realism in drama. Even if you don't know much about fifth-century Greece, the clash of cultures and personalities that we call the Persian Wars (499-449BC) has been the subject of popular entertainment in movies like *The 300 Spartans* (1962) and *300* (2006). The separate and very different Greek city-states (mostly) united against the Persian empire, which sought to spread west. The Persians were profoundly different to the Greeks in language, culture, government, and military strength and it seemed unlikely that Greece would overcome them. Yet they did, and the reasons for this moved Herodotus (who was born during the wars in Halicarnassus, a Greek city in Asia Minor then part of the Persian empire), to write the first European work of history.

A fragment of Herodotus' work discovered in the nineteenth century near Oxyrhynchus in Egypt. The transmission of texts and versions of ancient texts is a major problem in historiography.

What differentiated Herodotus and Thucydides from previous writers about the past – what makes them 'historians' – was this: they believed that writing about the past could be done for reasons other than theological or dynastic. For the first time, an investigation into the past was led by the belief that we could write down accurately what had really happened and suggest causes and outcomes that were based in the physical or psychological world.

Herodotus tells us that his main aim was to understand the events that had made a small Greek *polis* important and permitted the extraordinary development of Athenian democracy. His secondary aim was to ensure that

> what human beings have done will not fade through the passage of time and ... that the great and amazing actions of the Greeks and the Barbarians will not lose their fame, and in particular the reason why they went to war against one another.

Herodotus described his work as an *istoria*, or enquiry, showing an intellectual open-mindedness which we recognize from the Platonic dialogues. Also unusual was Herodotus' recognition that equally critically-minded readers would want to check what he said, or at least to see where he had obtained his information. Thus he wrote extensively about the journeys he had taken to amass his material, frequently naming and evaluating his sources. The world as Herodotus knew it was quite circumscribed, but it is likely that he visited a great deal of it, at a pace and in a manner almost impossible today. This, together with a developing habit of scepticism and interrogation, communicated in the plain and clear prose, which was becoming preferred in his intellectual environment, culminated in a new type of writing that we now call history.

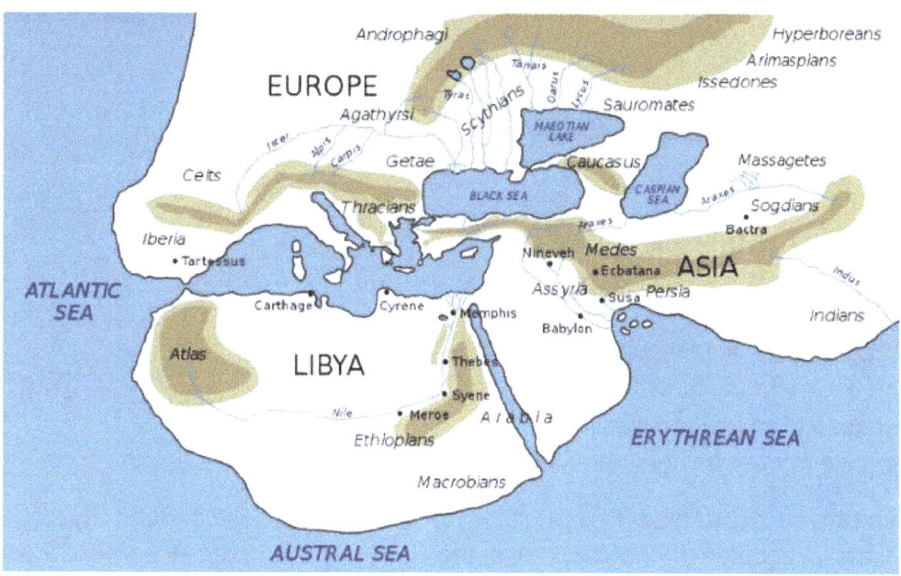

The world according to Herodotus, c. 450 BC. He personally went as far west as Rome, and probably as far east as Assyria; as far north as the northern shores of the Black Sea and as far south as Elephantine on the southern Nile.

As Gaston Basile says, 'the term *historia* does not designate a specific genre dealing with the human past but rather a novel cognitive category and discursive form.' By treating the stories which he heard as sources answering a question, rather than partisan products which supported or outraged his personal bias, Herodotus could write respectfully about the Persians' culture and political motives. His inclusion of stories from religion, myth, culture, and personal experience make his work far broader in scope than what we might think history normally covers. This is Herodotus' point, though: all facets of life are relevant to historical questions, and nothing is 'beneath' a historian's notice.

CONCEPT FOCUS 1: HISTORICAL CONSCIOUSNESS

Traditionally, Herodotus has been seen as a unique and highly idiosyncratic individual who single-handedly brought about the genre of 'history.' Research into the Greek prose-writers who preceded him now shows that Herodotus may have been the epigone of this style of writing and thinking, but he was not the sole exponent. Rather, he stands at the peak of a long chain of evolving styles of writing and thinking about tradition, narrative, the past, and the practice of asking questions.

Read the following extracts from different texts and discuss how they reflect a transition towards historical consciousness.

1. The earliest record of a past event is the **Stele of the Vultures** from Mesopotamia. It is dated to around 2600-2350 BCE and commemorates a victory of the city of Lagash over its neighbour Umma. It is preserved only in fragments, but a discernible historical narrative is present, in which the progress of the two cities' dispute over boundaries is very clear.

> ... its subsistence rations he {the king of Umma} reduced.
> Its grain rent he took away.
> The king of Lagash
> […]
> In the ... of ...
> the ruler of Umma, an aggressive act
> he committed against it,
> and into Lagash, up to its frontier
> he pressed.
> Akurgal, king of Lagash,
> son of Ur-Nanshe, king of Lagash,
> […]
> The ruler of Umma
> an aggressive act he committed against it,
> and into Lagash,
> because of its own possessions,
> up to its frontier he again pressed.

2. **The Annals of Thutmose III** are dated to around 1458-1438 BCE. By contrast, the Chinese annalist tradition did not begin until the *Spring and Autumn Annals* of 722-481 BCE. The Annals of Thutmose were inscribed on a section of wall in the 'Holy of Holies' in the temple at Karnak, and would not have been seen by the general public.

> Horus: Strong-Bull-arisen-in-Thebes; [Two Ladies: Enduring--in-kingship-like-Re-in-heaven; Gold-Horus: Mighty-in-strength, Ma-jestic-in-appearance]; the King of Upper and Lower Egypt, Lord of the Two Lands: Menkheperre; the Son of Re, [of his body: Tuthmosis, given life forever]. His majesty commanded to record [the victories his father Amun had given him] by an inscription in the temple which his majesty had made for [his father Amun, so as to record] each campaign, together with the booty which [his majesty] had brought [from it, and the tribute of every foreign land] that his father Re had given him. Year 22, fourth month of winter, day 25, [his majesty passed the fortress of] Sile on the first campaign of victory [to smite those who attacked]

the borders of Egypt, in valour [strength, might, and right]. For a [long] period of years ------ plunder, with every man [serving] ---. For it had happened in the time of other (kings) that the garrison there was (only) in Sharuhen, while from Yerdj to the ends of the earth there was rebellion against his majesty.

3. Nearly a millennium later is the **Behistun Inscription**, produced 521-486 BC in the cliffs of Mount Bisitun in Iran (*left*). It is written in Old Persian, Elamite, and Babylonian. It takes the form of a speech by Darius I, the Persian Emperor who commenced the war against Greece which his son, Xerxes, would conclude (by losing), and about whose life Herodotus writes. The inscription is an example of writing about past events which preceded Herodotus' work, in another (but related) culture. The first section of the inscription begins:

> King Darius says: My father is Hystaspes; the father of Hystaspes was Arsames; the father of Arsames was Ariaramnes; the father of Ariaramnes was Teispes; the father of Teispes was Achaemenes. King Darius says: That is why we are called Achaemenids; from antiquity we have been noble; from antiquity has our dynasty been royal. King Darius says: Eight of my dynasty were kings before me; I am the ninth. Nine in succession we have been kings.

> King Darius says: By the grace of Ahuramazda am I king; Ahuramazda has granted me the kingdom.

4. In the generation just before Herodotus, the writer **Hecataeus of Miletus** (b. 550BC) set about examining the mythic and epic traditions with a critical and rationalizing stance. Unfortunately, much of his work *Genealogies* is lost, but the opening statement of his proem has been preserved:

> Hecataeus of Miletus speaks thus: I write these words as they seem to me to be true; for the stories of the Greeks, as they seem to me, are many and ludicrous.

5. The divine origins of ruling families, and the interventions of the gods in significant events are questioned in fairly plain prose, which combines skepticism about causes with prose-narrative and a distinctly personal voice, in Protagoras' **Peri Theon**:

> About the gods I am not able to know neither that they exist nor that they do not exist nor of what kind they are in form: for many things prevent me from knowing this, its obscurity and the brevity of man's life.

Herodotus may have known of Hecataeus' work and perhaps that of Protagoras. He certainly knew Sophocles, whose plays were part of a festival of drama in which mythical, recent, and current events were considered ripe for subjective representation of varying degrees of accuracy. While Herodotus' work is unique in its scope, vigour, and charm, he has even more value as an example of the evolution of thinking and writing in a culture.

The fundamental components of historical writing are: an individual author; a question; an investigation; sources, and a narrative.

Thucydidean Responses

A generation after Herodotus' story of Greek resistance to Persia, Thucydides wrote about the aftermath – the Peloponnesian Wars, in which the Athenian and Spartan leagues warred over hegemony of Greece. His 'tragic' recount of internal conflict and Athenian political ambition was even more single-minded in reconstructing an accurate story of the past. Thucydides was openly critical of mixing fables with verifiable fact. He did not doubt that the story of the war between Athens and the rival states led by Sparta was worth recording, but he only told part of the story, mostly restricted to war and politics. Disinterested in rhetorical flourishes, Thucydides wrote in a terse and clear style which is reckoned by some to be 'a model for serious history writing.'

Thucydides says less than Herodotus about his sources but he assured readers that he had included only what he had witnessed himself or had been reported to him by reliable witnesses. Although more limited in scope than Herodotus, Thucydides' story of the Peloponnesian Wars still provides a model for military and political history. He includes speeches by leading participants in the wars, which (although he personally heard many of them) he did not transcribe verbatim:

> my method has been, while keeping as closely as possible to the general sense of the words that were actually used, to make the speakers say what, in my opinion, was called for by each situation.

A famous example is Pericles' Funeral Oration, which was used as a model for rhetoricians for over 1800 years. What we read is, therefore, a 'gist' or approximation of what Thucydides remembers those speakers having said. It was not until the 18th century that historians began to object to such 'dramatization' or fictionalization of events which the writer claimed were presented accurately. This reminds us that it took over two millenia for historiography to assert that there were problems involved in using literary fictions in order to make history more interesting or convincing.

Although Herodotus' *Histories* and Thucydides' *The Peloponnesian War* represent different but equally compelling visions of how history should be written, both adopted narrative as the most appropriate form. By using parchment or papyrus instead of an oral tradition, they could influence readers long after their own deaths. They could reach a relatively widely-dispersed audience, and their work could be compared to other writings. This allowed people to see clearly and critically the challenges of recording past events and people. They also regarded history with a pragmatic view, as 'useful' in instructing people about what had worked in certain situation, and what hadn't. Not only was this good instruction in war and statecraft, but it constructed a view of human action as flexible, open to change, and ordered by the will. Although this could pose its own problems, the position that we are responsible for our own actions has greatly contributed to the character of Western, individualist society.

2. What benefits and problems can you see with the pragmatic approach to history?

_____

_____

_____

Despite being 'lost' during the Middle Ages, these historians were 'rediscovered' during the European Renaissance and became regarded as the foundations of the Western historical tradition. Herodotus and Thucydides provided models for every Western historian after them, even those working in other media such as historical films, where script-writing can be seen as part of that ancient tradition.

Think laterally

Herodotus told a story with lots of rhetorical flourishes and a wide focus, and Thucydides had a pared-back style and inserted speeches focusing on politics and wars.

3. What type of reading environment suited the two kinds of History-writing?

4. Suggest how their societies would have received the work of Herodotus and Thucydides.

5. Historical movies are one type of historical medium. Suggest some others.

Polybius and Livy

The Romans greatly admired the Greek tradition of history-writing. Latin-language historians became better-known and more influential than either Herodotus or Thucydides because educated Europeans were more likely to read Latin until well into the twentieth century.

In the mid-second century BC, Polybius (203-120 BC) sought to explain the rise of Rome over a period of several centuries. The scope of Polybius' work is important: Herodotus and Thucydides had only covered events during their lifetime or the recent past (the mythical stories which Herodotus includes were part of a common oral fund which living people continued from one generation to the next). Their reliance on eye-witness accounts meant that their perspective was very short: they couldn't ask questions about events beyond living memory. As Collingwood said, the historian was 'only the autobiographer of his generation.' This also made it very difficult for later historians to interrogate or improve a history which had already been written, because the sources weren't available to them – that is, the people whom the first historian had used as sources were all dead. This meant that for critical history writing to occur, a number of 'generation-biographies' had to be written, so that they could then be compared, contrasted, and used selectively. Although this has been called the 'scissors-and-paste' method, it was almost the only way that critical history could come into being.

Polybius employed the narrative style already forged by Herodotus and Thucydides, having first collected and evaluated sources (often legal texts) from Rome's distant past. Like his Greek predecessors, Polybius recognised the difficulty of separating fact from fable and of reconciling different chronologies. Where the Greeks had employed a four-yearly chronology based on the Olympiad, the Romans had at least two different systems: one that calculated dates from the city's traditional foundation in 753 BC; the other according to the names of the annually elected consuls.

Despite these challenges, Polybius justified his project by saying that

> what is really educational and beneficial to students of history is the clear view of the causes of events and the consequent power of choosing the best policy in a particular cause.

In a way, Polybius advances Thucydides' 'tragic' view of the ambitious state, by seeking to clarify why states fail, and whether this is a universal law. Rome's unique combination of monarchy, aristocracy, and democracy had given it a greater lifespan, but Polybius felt that, by the time he was writing, Rome's decline was undeniable. This introduces an interesting tension in his narrative, between the elements of political and moral utility for the future, and the pessimistic perspective which suggests that it will fail nonetheless. Polybius thus gave the discipline two important elements: one was a focus on the reasons for the Roman republic's extraordinary success and its replacement by autocracy; the second was a framework of decline and pessimism which has influenced politics and history writing, especially since the Renaissance.

Polybius' successors, Livy (59 BC-17 AD) and Tacitus (54-120 AD), also took up the task of explaining conflict and the sense of decline by considering how Rome abandoned its unique amalgam of institutions. Livy's enormously ambitious history (which only survives in fragments, although these are extremely lengthy) drew on mythic thinking to depict the far past as golden, heroic, and rigorous, in contrast with his own disappointing time. Tacitus portrayed the emperors' corrupt, *superbia*-laden actions with an overtly moral purpose: '...to record merit and threaten evil deeds and words with posterity's denunciation.'

This depiction of the Capitoline Wolf, suckling the brothers Romulus (the traditional founder of Rome) and Remus, was probably made around the 13th century AD, with the brothers being added in the 15th century. It shows the tenacity with which cultures hold on to certain myths, even when they conflict with the dominant thinking – in this case, European Christianity.

In the same era, the Greek writer Plutarch (46-120 AD) pioneered the form we recognise as biography, although his purpose was more subtle. Plutarch wrote parallel lives, pairing a famous Greek life with a famous Roman one, to draw out how great men reacted to similar pressures, and discern the apparent similarities underpinning 'greatness.' These were, however, often largely constructed by Plutarch's cutting and shaping of the biographical narrative.

By the end of the second century AD the tradition of historical writing was already 600 years old. Enough material had been written to allow practitioners to begin formulating a philosophy about their method. Cicero (106-43 BC) and Quintilian (35-100 AD) wrote about history's function and proper composition. Lucian of Samosata's (125-180 AD) *How to Write History* considered issues confronting historians even today. According to Lucian, the historian should be 'fearless, incorruptible, free… independent, subject to no sovereign, not reckoning what this or that man will think, but stating the facts.'

Although Lucian's words are laudable, readers should remember the significant practical limitations on historians (and their audiences) before the modern age. Not only were these limitations physical – until the invention of printing, most people would never handle a book let alone own one, and an even smaller number actually knew how to read one intelligently – they were cultural too. We are never free from biases, and even so-called rational secularists are biased, but the further back in history we go, the more pronounced is the presence of the supernatural and miraculous as a causal agent in historical explanation.

Think laterally

6. Suggest why Herodotus and Polybius were interested in accounting for the supremacy of a civilization.

7. What do you think is the difference between an educated person and a 'cultivated' one? Can you give examples of a cultivated person?

8. Suggest connections between having historical knowledge and being 'educated', and, likewise being 'cultivated'. What is the link between them and why do societies often stress this?

Extend yourself

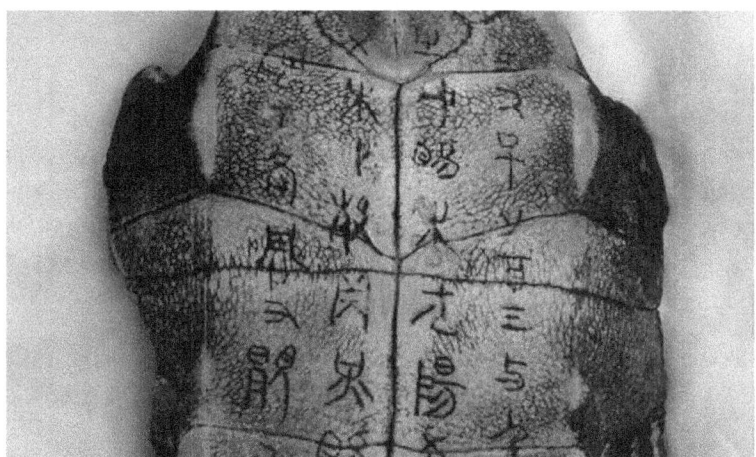

The first attempts to make a record of historical events in China date from the Shang dynasty (second millennium BC). The earliest surviving records were inscribed on bones or tortoise shells (*above*); in later centuries, chroniclers left detailed accounts on paper or silk. In the last hundred years, archaeologists have discovered a wealth of new materials, including a cache of previously-unknown texts found in a sealed cave on the edge of the Gobi Desert. Such sources are shedding new light on Chinese history, although interpreting ancient sources from the period before the invention of printing presents a number of challenges.

Somewhat earlier than Herodotus, Confucius chronicled several centuries of China's past in *Chungui* or 'Spring and Summer Annals'. In the same way that the *auctores* (famous authors) of the ancient West acquired a commentary tradition (called the *accessus ad auctores*) which made them more accessible and drew out the complications and contradictions in their work, there were many commentaries on *Chungui*.

In the second century BC Sima Qian compiled *Shiji*, an account of how the Han dynasty unified China after 206 BC. Rather like an encyclopaedia of dynastic culture, complete with chronological tables and separate biographies which remind us that the continuous narrative is not the only way to write history, *Shiji* recounted the various dynasties that had ruled China's regions for some 2000 years. Like Herodotus, Sima Qian included the roles played by women and he did not rigidly separate legends from documents, and like Thucydides, he also recognized that the study of the past had significant moral and political utility for the future.

Subsequently, the activity of narrating the past flourished in China. The Tang dynasty (618-906 AD) created an official History Bureau to demonstrate and document previous rulers' loss of the 'Mandate of Heaven' and so justify their overthrow. The subsequent Song Dynasty (960-1279 AD) continued to develop a sophisticated critique of historical method four hundred years before European attempts to do the same. In the 11th century Ouyang Xiu and Sima Guang explained the importance of archaeological evidence and inscriptions in corroborating written sources. They also insisted on the superiority of written sources written close to the time of past events.

One excellent source of information about Sima Qian is a BBC podcast from a series called *As History is My Witness*. You should be able to find the podcast by looking up the series title.

Extend yourself

9. The concept of truth is much more complicated than it appears. Several major theories of truth are important to historians. These are: Correspondence theory; Coherence theory; Deflationary theory, and Pragmatic theory. Research these (briefly – there is a vast amount of reading for each one) and write a brief definition of what they are and how they may apply to historical writing.

A good introduction is the BBC *In Our Time* series, presented by Melvyn Bragg. You should be able to find the podcast on Truth by searching for the series on the BBC website.

Notes

Reading task 1

Read this passage from the opening of Herodotus' *The History*.

The Persian learned men say that the Phoenicians were the cause of the feud. These (they say) came to our seas from the sea which is called Red, and having settled in the country which they still occupy, at once began to make long voyages. Among other places to which they carried Egyptian and Assyrian merchandise, they came to Argos, which was about that time pre-eminent in every way among the people of what is now called Hellas. The Phoenicians then came, as I say, to Argos, and set out their cargo. On the fifth or sixth day from their coming, their wares being now well-nigh all sold, there came to the sea shore among many other women the king's daughter, whose name (according to Persians and Greeks alike) was Io, the daughter of Inachus. They stood about the stern of the ship: and while they bargained for such wares as they fancied, the Phoenicians heartened each other to the deed, and rushed to take them. Most of the women escaped: Io with others was carried off; the men cast her into the ship and made sail away for Egypt.

This, say the Persians (but not the Greeks), was how Io came to Egypt, and this, according to them, was the first wrong that was done. Next, according to their tale, certain Greeks (they cannot tell who) landed at Tyre in Phoenice and carried off the king's daughter Europe. These Greeks must, I suppose, have been Cretans. So far, then, the account between them stood balanced. But after this (they say), it was the Greeks who were guilty of the second wrong.

...

These are the stories of the Persians and the Phoenicians. For my own part, I will not say that this or that story is true, but I will name him whom I myself know to have done unprovoked wrong to the Greeks, and so go forward with my history, and speak of small and great cities alike. For many states that were once great have now become small: and those that were great in my time were small formerly. Knowing therefore that human prosperity never continues in one stay, I will make mention alike of both kinds.

1. Identify (by highlighting or underlining) the features of historiographical discourse discussed in Chapter 1 and list them below.

2. What features of writing style are evident in this passage?

3. Who might have read this work in Herodotus' time?

4. Why might someone read it now?

5. Cicero admitted that Herodotus was both the 'father of history' and the 'father of lies'. Based on your reading of this section, what is your reaction to this charge?

Chapter revision statement

It helps to list the key points from each chapter to synthesise your knowledge about historiography.

Once you've written a list of key points, compose a statement which includes all the items, and use it for revision before exams. We've completed this chapter's revision statement as an example.

The Habit of History: key points

1. A privileged male (pre)occupation
2. Mostly about war and politics
3. Hindered by multiple chronologies
4. Preoccupied by the rise and degeneration of powerful nations
5. Led by a question
6. And a strongly moral purpose
7. Creative liberties with factual accuracy
8. Opinions about the use and value of sources
9. A narrative

Revision statement

Ancient historians shaped the discipline until the 16th century. History was a narrative which answered a question, mostly about the success or decline of powerful nations, seen through their wars and politics. Written by privileged men who had strong opinions about the use and value of sources, history was given a moral purpose, although this didn't prevent historians from taking creative liberties with facts.

Notes

Chapter 2: Post-Classical history

The Greco-Roman tradition of historical writing, with its relatively rational and secular interest in politics and the large-scale causes of change such as governmental corruption and cultural decay, was significantly different to the Judeo-Christian view of history. Herodotus and Polybius had both been interested in causes: Polybius had developed a sophisticated concept of causality, but most ancient historians thought in terms of cycles of virtue and decadence.

Christian historians developed a new vision of the past based in theological teachings about the kingdom of God. While writers like Thucydides and Polybius believed that the rise and fall of empires lay in human actions, Jews and Christians added another level beyond, or behind, these actions. This level was divine and pre-existed the human beings who acted it out. The concept of a divine plan or *oeconomia* to which history conformed, and which would culminate in a Messianic return, was the 'grand narrative' of these initially relatively minor faith-groups. They drew on their own chronologically-oriented scriptures, particularly works of prophecy, and looked beyond their own time to the end of things. This was the first thorough-going teleological (or 'end-oriented,' from the Greek *telos* or end, aim) perspective, and it did not pretend to be unbiased.

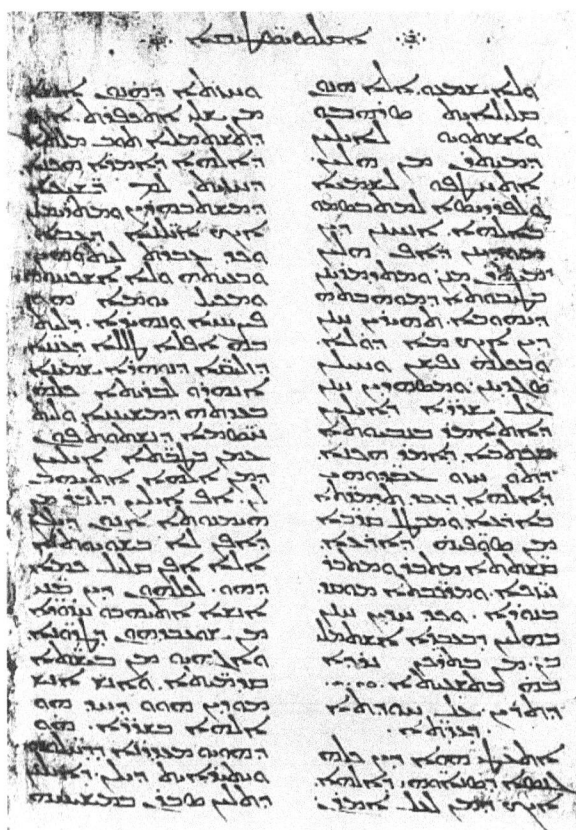

In 313AD the emperor Constantine issued the Edict of Milan which made Christianity the official creed of the Roman empire, and the Christian tenor and direction of written history became influential. Eusebius, bishop of Caesarea Maritima, developed an historical tradition that dominated the European worldview for more than a millennium. Published around 313 A.D., his *History of the Church* was the first narrative of the events after the apostolic diaspora contained in the letters of the New Testament and covered the period up to his own time. He wrote in Koine Greek, which implies a desire to have his work read by as large a population as possible, although it contains some significant use of rhetoric particularly in its treatment of supporters of the early Church. It was quickly translated into neighbouring languages, and the earliest manuscripts are Syriac (*left*). Largely polemical, Eusebius understood the importance of direct citation from sources and incorporated large tracts of other texts into his own material. Many of these texts were later lost, and survive only through Eusebius' incorporation. His *History of the Church* brought together three themes dominant in the content of Christian history: institutions; prophecy, and miracles.

In some ways, the acceptance of divine intervention seems a step backwards to the credulity of Herodotus, but Eusebius and other early Christian historians do not include these fantastic stories for narrative colour or rhetorical novelty: they are subordinate to the presence of the grand plan of which they are both proof and part. This plan, Christian historians believed, *intends* Christian institutions to flourish, and our understanding of the plan is at once intrinsically historical and literary, since early scripture is put forward as a series of promises of the events attested to by later scripture. Thus to have a complete grasp of the historicity of salvation one must have a solid grasp of the texts which recount it.

Illustration of a scene described in Eusebius' history: the emperor Constantine's vision of the cross before the Battle of the Milvian Bridge, which prompted his conversion to Christianity. This illustration is from a ninth-century manuscript of the homilies (sermons) of Gregory Nazianzus – not Eusebius' History.

Like many historians who preceded him, Eusebius makes a declaration of method at the beginning of his *History of the Church* which outlines the grouping of material according to the reigns of the emperors, and the different elements on which he will focus. It builds in a narrative way on an earlier work, his *Chronicle*, in which he attempted to give a comparative timeline of gentile and Old Testament history. (The *Chronicle* established the model for the chronicle-genre which became enormously popular in the Medieval period). In this early work we can already see that Eusebius regarded all past events as leading up to the Christian Era, and that the history of other nations and cultures was of secondary interest to the Old Testament and the history of the Chosen People, which became a kind of cultural-historical standard measurement. By doing this, Eusebius added chronology as an important skill to the study of history, and showed through his own work one way of harmonizing the many different chronological measurements in the Mediterranean.

Just as Eusebius' history was prompted by the changed status of Christianity after Constantine's Edict in 313 AD, Augustine's work *The City of God* was prompted by the sack of Rome by the Goths in 410 AD. Pagans felt that this catastrophe had occurred because the old gods objected to the new Christian faith, and Augustine spent thirteen years writing an enormous response which was at once a survey and criticism of Roman tradition and a vindication of Christianity. Although not a work of history *per se*, *The City of God* presents a philosophy of history: it explains past events on the basis of a universal principle. This principle was the separation of the earthly political state (the 'earthly city') and the divine institution of the faithful (the 'heavenly city'), a separation of powers and domains which has been observed in many different political forms since then. In this book Augustine propounded the relationship between Church and State, visible events and invisible plan, past and present – and perhaps also history and the philosophy of history.

But Christians wrote more than simply social or political history. The Christian faith rested on four documents of a uniquely personal character: each of the four canonical gospels (and many of the non-canonical gospels) reflects the interests and audience of its writer, and their personal experience of the 'good news' of individual salvation through the death and resurrection of the central figure. Augustine of Hippo, although not himself an historian, related the narrative of his own inner life in his *Confessions* around 400AD, in which he recorded his thoughts and feelings to accompany the narrative of external actions, thereby establishing the genre of autobiography.

Think laterally

The central plot in Christian History-writing is 'Fall and Redemption'. Fall and Redemption are shown to occur at different chronological times and places, but with increasing urgency until the end of time.

1. What do you think the central plot is for ONE of the pre-Christian historians you've heard about so far?

2. List the ways that autobiography is part of historical writing, and how it differs from History.

CONCEPT FOCUS 2: GRAND NARRATIVES

All writing is a subjective representation of the world which conveys both facts and the author's view of the significance or pattern which those facts hold. Historians frequently shape their account according to a 'grand narrative', an underlying ideology about how the world really is. This may have propagandistic elements: the Whig narrative of progress, or the Enlightenment narrative of the triumph of rational secular democracy, are examples. Identify how the grand narratives are made evident in these short extracts.

Herodotus: Greek as the norm, Persian as Other

"O king [Xerxes]," said Demaratus, "seeing that you bid me by all means speak the whole truth, and say that which you shall not afterwards prove to be false, — in Hellas poverty is ever native to the soil, but courage comes of their own seeking, the fruit of wisdom and strong law; by use of courage Hellas defends herself from poverty and tyranny. Now I say nought but good of all Greeks that dwell in those Dorian lands; yet it is not of all that I would now speak, but only of Lacedaemonians; and this I say of them; firstly, that they will never accept conditions from you that import the enslaving of Hellas; and secondly, that they will meet you in battle, yea, even though all the rest of the Greeks be on your side. But, for the number of them, ask me not how many these men are, who are like to do as I say; be it of a thousand men, or of more or of fewer than that, their army will fight with you."

Polybius: The inevitability of moral decline

Such is the cycle of political revolution, the course appointed by nature in which constitutions change, disappear, and finally return to the point from which they started. Anyone who clearly perceives this may indeed in speaking of the future of any state be wrong in his estimate of the time the process will take, but if his judgement is not tainted by animosity or jealousy, he will very seldom be mistaken as to the stage of growth or decline it has reached, and as to the form into which it will change. And especially in the case of the Roman state will this method enable us to arrive at a knowledge of its formation, growth, and greatest perfection, and likewise of the change for the worse which is sure to follow some day. For, as I said, this state, more than any other, has been formed and has grown naturally, and will undergo a natural decline and change to its contrary. The reader will be able to judge of the truth of this from the subsequent parts of this work.

Livy: The inevitability of moral decline

The subjects to which I would ask each of my readers to devote his earnest attention are these-the life and morals of the community; the men and the qualities by which through domestic policy and foreign war dominion was won and extended. Then as the standard of morality gradually lowers, let him follow the decay of the national character, observing how at first it slowly sinks, then slips downward more and more rapidly, and finally begins to plunge into headlong ruin, until he reaches these days, in which we can bear neither our diseases nor their remedies.

Augustine: The providential plan of salvation

How could these, and whatever like things are found in the Roman history, have become so widely known, and have been proclaimed by so great a fame, had not the Roman empire, extending far and wide, been raised to its greatness by magnificent successes? Wherefore, through that empire, so extensive and of so long continuance, so illustrious and glorious also through the virtues of such great men, the reward which they sought was rendered to their earnest aspirations, and also examples are set before us, containing necessary admonition, in order that we may be stung with shame if we shall see that we have not held fast those virtues for the sake of the most glorious city of God, which are, in whatever way, resembled by those virtues which they held fast for the sake of the glory of a terrestrial city, and that, too, if we shall feel conscious that we have held them fast, we may not be lifted up with pride, because, as the apostle says, The sufferings of the present time are not worthy to be compared to the glory which shall be revealed in us.

Eusebius: The providential plan of salvation

For which of the kings who ever lived achieved such greatness as to fill the ears and mouths of all men on earth with his name? What king established laws so just and impartial, and was strong enough to have them proclaimed in the hearing of all mankind from the ends of the earth and to the furthest limit of the entire world? Who made the barbarous, uncivilized customs of uncivilized races give place to his own civilized and most humane laws? Who was for whole ages attacked on every side, yet displayed such superhuman greatness as to be for ever in his prime and to remain young throughout his life? Who so firmly established a people unheard-of from the beginning of time that it is not hidden in some corner of the earth but is found in every place under the sun? Who so armed his soldiers with the weapons of true religion that their souls proved tougher than steel in their battles with their opponents? Which of the kings wields such power, leads his armies after death, sets up trophies over his enemies, and fills every place, district, and city, Greek or non-Greek, with votive offerings - his own royal houses and sacred temples, like this cathedral with its exquisite ornaments and offerings?

Bede: The providential plan of salvation

Thus the aforesaid Pope Boniface wrote for the salvation of King Edwin and his nation. But a heavenly vision, which the Divine Mercy was pleased once to reveal to this king, when he was in banishment at the court of Redwald, king of the Angles, was of no little use in urging him to embrace and understand the doctrines of salvation. Paulinus, therefore, perceiving that it was a very difficult task to incline the king's lofty mind to the humility of the way of salvation, and to embrace the mystery of the cross of life, and at the same time using both exhortation with men, and prayer to God, for his and his subjects' salvation; at length, as we may suppose, it was shown him in spirit what was the vision that had been formerly revealed to the king. Nor did he lose any time, but immediately admonished the king to perform the vow which he made, when he received the oracle, promising to put the same in execution, if he was delivered from the trouble he was at that time under, and should be advanced to the throne.

Anonymous Italian Jew in spring 1495: Tribulations of the Chosen People

And in the year 5252 [1492], in the days of King Ferdinand, the Lord visited the remnant of his people a second time [the first Spanish visitation was in 1391], and exiled them. After the King had captured the city of Granada from the Moors, and it had surrendered to him on the 7th [2d] of January of the year just mentioned, he ordered the expulsion of all the Jews in all parts of his kingdom...Even before that the Queen had expelled them from the kingdom of Andalusia [1483].

History in the Middle Ages

For many centuries medieval history-writing was regarded as dull, disconnected, naïve, and parochial. Because chronicles tended to display both the Christian interest in the morality of actions and an obsession with chronology, much of the history written in the period 800-1400 seems lacklustre compared to the intellectual dynamic of the Renaissance. Yet recent historiographers have offered a more nuanced understanding of mediaeval historians' motives, and their capacity to live locally while thinking universally. The best example is the writing of Bishop Gregory of Tours (528-594), whose *History of the Franks* is one of the first histories of an ethnic and cultural people, as opposed to a city, city-state, or empire. Gregory recorded contemporary history to persuade his readers of his pastoral ideas. His Latin is sometimes very shaky but his stories are extremely colourful, and the work is a highly-readable mixture of stories, some about local people, others about the great and powerful. His *History* remains one of the most comprehensive depictions of life in the pre-modern world.

But perhaps the most important contribution to historical writing in this period was the *Ecclesiastical History of the English People* written by a monk from the Northumbrian monastery at Jarrow called Bede (672/3 – 26 May 735). Bede's history is a great work of scholarship, not only because of his careful and conscious use of sources, but because of his elegant interweaving of three historical strands into a single perspective. It is the history of an institution - the English church, as opposed to the Celtic church. It is also a history of a people – the 'English' people who inhabited some of the southern British isles before the waves of Saxon migrants came from Europe. And it is the history of an idea – that the feast of Easter was of such importance that differences in dating it constituted an unbridgeable gap between religious communities. It is a highly detailed account of the struggle between the Roman and Celtic churches in England, with the Synod of Whitby acting as the high-point of the narrative. Bede's highly organized, elegant writing encompassed a concern for factual accuracy, a careful treatment of his sources, and a consistent and novel method of chronology. Bede was the first to use Jesus of Nazareth's birth as a chronological place-holder, dividing time into years *Before Christ* and *Anno Domini*, and so cementing the idea of the salvation *oeconomia* into cognitive structures in a very profound way. Nonetheless, Bede's history is dense in style and highly academic in tenor, and would have appealed mostly to clerics - who were also likely the only people to have access to a manuscript copy.

In the many dynastic controversies which happened during that period we came to call the 'Middle Ages', histories were often consulted for information about royal and noble lineages and inheritance. Because most of the writers were monastic, and monasteries were – as far as possible – protected during times of war, manuscript copies of histories, chronicles, and important documents were often kept in monastic repositories where they remained relatively safe. This is not to say that monastic historians were above falsifying or confabulating historical narratives. The British historian 12th-century historian Geoffrey of Monmouth wrote an extremely popular work called the *History of the Kings of Britain*, which traced the lineage of British kings to Brutus the Trojan, King Lear, and Arthur. Even his contemporaries were fairly unconvinced by Geoffrey's claims, but in the absence of any other comprehensive narrative, it was frequently taken as authoritative. More to the point, it said, in narrative terms with at least a veneer of plausibility, what important people either wanted to hear or generally believed. Many medieval forgeries and confabulations were of this nature: they were composed in order to give some textual form to a state of affairs which was generally believed to be true. It was simply inconvenient that solid evidence was lacking; the chronicler provided the 'evidence' and so solved the problem. Perhaps the most famous example of such 'creative' problem-solving was the Donation of Constantine, an imperial decree by which Constantine gave authority over Rome and the western empire to the Pope. In fact, it was probably composed in the eighth century and was declared to be a forgery by Otto of Freising in his history, written around 1147 AD, *The Two Cities*.

In the absence of any competing narrative, it was easier to accept the extant one as authoritative, even if it was patently dubious. When Edward I invaded Scotland in the 1290s with an eye to the Scottish throne, one of his first actions was to remove Scottish records and registers from families and monasteries. Their return was one of the clauses of the Treaty of Northampton in 1329, but the records remained in London until 1948 – when only around 200 of the several thousand were returned.

An illumination from a 15th-century manuscript of Geoffrey's work, showing two dragons fighting while king Vortigern looks on. The expense of this manuscript indicates the work's continued popularity, well after other historians had put forward competing narratives.

Historians after Geoffrey were quite capable of demonstrating skepticism about his narrative. Ranulph Higden, author of the mid-14th century *Polychronicon*, both pointed out Geoffrey's implausibilities and located the reason for them in the reader's psychology:

> Many men wonder about this Arthur, for it is only Geoffrey among all the chroniclers who praises him so much, and they ask how it is possible to know the truth about the things which are said of him. For according to Geoffrey he conquered thirty kingdoms...[yet] the chroniclers of Rome, of France, or the Saxons say nothing about such a great man. ... it seems that the custom is for each nation to extol beyond reason one of their own people. ...Thus did the Britons extol Arthur, and they do this as Josephus explains, partly to enjoy a good story, partly to please their readers, and partly to exalt their own blood.

Not all histories were as lively as those of Gregory and Geoffrey. The dry, laconic nature of many chronicles and their methodological failings – their unwillingness to use women's evidence, for example – may explain the popularity of later mediaeval works such as Jacobus de Voragine's massively popular *Golden Legend* (c. 1260), an anthology of saints' lives which was in some respects similar to Herodotus' tradition of mixing legends with historical narrative. Yet as the Middle Ages came to an end, a secular tradition of history-writing began to develop, where secular clerks, soldiers, diplomats, and even lay women began to produce accounts of events which they had experienced, and which they perceived as 'historic'. Two of the most important events of the period, the depositions of Edward II and Richard II, were described by secular eyewitnesses in accounts of great emotional power and historical importance and events in battle, the army camp, and in captivity were recounted by men who had actually experienced them. The soldier and poet Jean Froissart (1337-1405), claimed that:

> the greatest pleasure I have ever had was to make every possible inquiry in regard to what was passing in the world and then write down all that I had learned.

Froissart composed a long Arthurian romance and wrote a chronicle of his experiences in the Hundred Years War (1337-1453); historians of chivalry use his plain, clear narrative of secular events to gauge the reality of chivalric values, compared to the mythos which surrounds them.

Although it may seem strange to us, one claim which is made continually in medieval history is that of truthfulness which, as Chris Given-Wilson has pointed out, could mean accuracy, significance, *and* conformity to accepted values. With the growth of consultative bodies like parliaments, written records and accounts were increasingly called on to provide evidence and detail, making the secular clerks who wrote them very concerned with getting their facts right. This led, slowly but very surely, to a trend which has become almost synonymous with academic writing: that of referencing. Just as ancient historians constructed a parallel narrative of how they went about finding an answer to their questions, and Christian historians introduced the element of strict chronological reckoning, medieval historians added the truth claim and the reference to the growing toolkit of historical writing.

Jewish and Islamic Historians

Another development in history writing emerged after the Crusades which began in 1096, and is found in the writing by minority groups. Their experiences are often obscured by the 'grand narratives' which cast them as 'Other'. Jews established what Salo Wittmayer Baron called the 'lachrymose' tradition, the recounting of events from the perspective of victims rather than conquerors. On the basis of these accounts, later Jewish historians wrote histories which strove to give a fuller picture of life in societies with Jewish populations, by including those groups which had always been 'written out' of orthodox, gentile history. The lachrymose tradition can also be seen as the forerunner of a more recent 'testimonial' turn in twentieth-century history writing. The tradition of *temoinage* has exploded since the Second World War, particularly through institutions like Yad Vashem in Israel which aim to collect and preserve this body of testimony.

Islamic culture also quickly developed a tradition of sophisticated historical writing. Just as Christianity was deeply concerned with chronology because it measured progress towards the messianic return, the basis of Islamic faith and society was the authority of the Prophet's words. The Hadith tradition, which records the words and actions of Mohammed, developed its own system of chronology based on the flight to Medina in 622, called the *hijira*. It also included *isnad,* a systematic approach to the evaluation of proof, sources, and evidence, and like Christianity and Judaism, a legal system which was an offshoot of this historical, text-based thought.

Ibn Khaldun was a North African statesman who wrote one of the most important studies of the discipline of history. Khaldun was born in Tunis in 1332 and received a good education, but at the age of sixteen he lost many of his family to the Black Death. His adult life was similarly characterised by sharp turns of fortune: he built a career as a political operator in cities from Fez to Granada but often fared badly in court intrigues, and was imprisoned after failing to prevent the murder of a fellow statesman. In 1375, he withdrew into the Sahara to contemplate why the Muslim world had degenerated into division and decline. Four years later he had completed the *Muqaddimah*, not only a history of North African politics but also, in the book's long introduction, one of the great studies of history as a discipline.

In the *Muqaddimah* Khaldun identified seven principal errors which he felt historians often committed:

1. Simple bias towards a creed or view
2. Belief that one's source cannot be wrong, or has greater weight than it does
3. Taking something the wrong way, or in a way other than what was intended
4. Simple error in believing something is true when it is false. Khaldun noted also that documents are vulnerable to these errors
5. Ignoring the context of an event and its influence
6. Flattery of one's patron, or the desire to flatter a potential patron
7. Ignorance of the laws of change in society

Drawing on both regional history and personal experience, he set out a bleak analysis of the rise and fall of dynasties. He argued that group solidarity was vital to success in power. But within five generations, he noted, this always decayed. Tired urban dynasties inevitably became vulnerable to overthrow by rural insurgents. Later in life, Ibn Khaldun worked as a judge in Egypt, and in 1401 he met the terrifying Mongol conqueror Tamburlaine whose triumphs, Ibn Khaldun felt, bore out his own pessimistic theories. Over the last three centuries, Ibn Khaldun has been rediscovered as a profoundly prescient political scientist, philosopher of history and forerunner of sociology.

Think laterally

3. What force do you believe orders events (if any)? For example, English is the most widely-spoken language in the world, and anglophone culture undeniably the most proliferant in human history – so who or what has brought this about?

4. What assumptions does *temoinage* make in its narrative?

5. Look up Ibn Khaldun's famous list of errors. Most of them are mutually self-supporting. Choose TWO and explain how they might act in a historian's writing to exacerbate each other.

Extend yourself

There is an excellent podcast on Ibn Khaldun in the BBC *In Our Time* series. You should be able to find the podcast by searching for the series on the BBC website.

Notes

Reading task 2

Read the following passage from Eusebius' *Ecclesiastical History*.

It is my purpose to write an account of the lines of succession of the holy apostles, as well as of the times that have elapsed from the days of our Saviour to our own; and to relate the many important events that are said to have occurred in the history of the Church; and to mention those who have governed and presided over the Church in the most prominent parishes, and those who in each generation have proclaimed the divine word either orally or in writing.

It is my purpose also to give the names and number and dates of those who through love of innovation have run into the greatest errors, and, proclaiming themselves discoverers of knowledge falsely so-called (1 Timothy 6:20) have like fierce wolves mercilessly devastated the flock of Christ.

It is my intention, moreover, to recount the misfortunes that immediately came upon the whole Jewish nation in consequence of their plots against our Saviour, and to record the ways and the times in which the divine word has been attacked by the Gentiles, and to describe the character of those who at various periods have contended for it in the face of blood and of tortures, as well as the confessions which have been made in our own days, and finally the gracious and kindly succor which our Saviour has afforded them all. Since I propose to write of all these things I shall commence my work with the beginning of the dispensation of our Saviour and Lord Jesus Christ.

…

Others who composed historical narratives would simply have handed down in writing victories in wars and trophies against enemies and the prizes of generals and the bravery of hoplites stained with blood and numerous murders for the sake of children and country and other advantage. Yet the narrative account by us of the community of God's followers will record peaceful wars contested for peace itself in the soul, wars among them for the sake of truth rather than country and for religious devotion rather than even the most loved ones, on permanent stelae, proclaiming the resolve and sought-after prizes of athletes for religious devotion, trophies against demons, victories against unseen adversaries, and crowns in all these contests, to the perpetual remembrance.

…

After the death of Tiberius, Caius received the empire, and, besides innumerable other acts of tyranny against many people, he greatly afflicted especially the whole nation of the Jews. These things we may learn briefly from the words of Philo, who writes as follows:

So great was the caprice of Caius in his conduct toward all, and especially toward the nation of the Jews. The latter he so bitterly hated that he appropriated to himself their places of worship in the other cities, and beginning with Alexandria he filled them with images and statues of himself (for in permitting others to erect them he really erected them himself). The temple in the holy city, which had hitherto been left untouched, and had been regarded as an inviolable asylum, he altered and transformed into a temple of his own, that it might be called the temple of the visible Jupiter, the younger Caius.

Innumerable other terrible and almost indescribable calamities which came upon the Jews in Alexandria during the reign of the same emperor, are recorded by the same author in a second work, to which he gave the title *On the Virtues*. With him agrees also Josephus, who likewise indicates that the misfortunes of the whole nation began with the time of Pilate, and with their daring crimes against the Saviour.

Hear what he says in the second book of his Jewish War, where he writes as follows: Pilate being sent to Judea as procurator by Tiberius, secretly carried veiled images of the emperor, called ensigns, to Jerusalem by night. The following day this caused the greatest disturbance among the Jews. For those who were near were confounded at the sight, beholding their laws, as it were, trampled underfoot. For they allow no image to be set up in their city.

Comparing these things with the writings of the evangelists, you will see that it was not long before there came upon them the penalty for the exclamation which they had uttered under the same Pilate, when they cried out that they had no other king than Cæsar. (John 19:15)

1. Identify (by highlighting or underlining) the features of Christian historiographical discourse discussed in this chapter.

2. According to Eusebius, what forces underlie events and cause them to happen?

___

3. Compare this extract with Herodotus, in Reading task 1. What similarities and differences are evident?

___

4. In what ways does Eusebius use other writers' work within the body of his own text?

Notes

Chapter revision statement

Write a list of the key points from this chapter.

_____
_____
_____
_____
_____
_____
_____
_____
_____
_____

Use the list to write a short statement about important features in the discipline of History during the period studied in this chapter.

_____
_____
_____
_____
_____
_____
_____

Notes

_____
_____
_____
_____
_____
_____
_____
_____
_____
_____

Chapter 3: Renaissance and Reformation

The practice of history, or narrative reconstructions of people and past events, was greatly affected by the transformations of the 'Four Rs': Renaissance; Reconnaissance; Reformation and Revolution. These four forces combined to create what is often called the 'Early Modern Era' (as distinct from the Middle Ages and the Modern Era).

Recovery of Written Texts

Having fractured into a number of city-states, the republics and kingdoms of Italy were variously equipped to continue the tradition of historical writing – or to break with it. In the cities which were relatively free from papal influence, new sub-disciplines began to surface which provided impetus for a new way of thinking about the past.

For one thing, there was a new recognition of what Herbert Butterfield has called 'the sheer pastness of things past.' Having ignored or recycled the physical past (in the form of buildings and manuscripts) for their own purposes, Italians began to take a scholarly interest in the past. There was a sense that so much past had to be divided into manageable categories, according to the different values and tenor of the times. Accordingly, Leonardo Bruni, Chancellor of Florence and apostolic secretary to four popes, used a new tripartite concept of history: Antiquity; the Middle Ages, and the Modern Age. This approach to time was unusually secular, but it was also politically motivated. Bruni took up the now-classic narrative of decline, to suggest that Italy had improved in recent centuries after a long 'Dark Age' and was returning to something like the vigour of the Roman republic. Described as the first modern historian, Bruni's work yoked together a secular view of time, an interest in republican politics, and a thorough knowledge of both Latin and Greek texts, culminating in what came to be called 'civic humanism'.

Flavio Biondo followed Bruni's use of a three-period division of the past, and his *History from the Decline of the Roman Empire* takes both a long view and a gloomy one, to which Edward Gibbon's epic *The Decline and Fall of the Roman Empire* would be much indebted. Biondo was, however, also interested in the physical past and was one of the first archaeologists. Like Biondo, Lorenzo de Medici collected together items distinguished by their age and displayed them in an arrangement called a 'museum'. Poggio Braccionlini, another Florentine, was a codicologist who discovered many ancient works in the libraries of European monasteries. Among his finds were: Lucretius' *De rerum natura*; Vitruvius' *De Architectura*; Ammanius Marcellinus' *Res Gestae*, and Quintilian's *Institutio Oratoriae*. Bracciolini was one of a circle of Florentine men who are now famous as 'Humanists' – men who regarded the learning of classical antiquity as the pinnacle of what was both beautiful and useful, and who sought to inject the same spirit in their own time. This scholarly interest was also quite secular: the insistence on divine plans underpinning historical events, and the moral character of the principal actors did not interest the European humanists at all.

One of the most important discoveries of the period had been made by the fourteenth-century polymath Francesco Petrarca, who found Cicero's letters in the chapter library of Verona Cathedral, a discovery which is often credited with kick-starting the Italian Renaissance. In historiographical terms, Petraca's discovery was important because it attracted the attention of Lorenzo Valla, a Roman lawyer who worked for the papal chancery.

Valla was a talented student of Latin and Greek, but he caused offence to many people with his criticism of their Latin style and rhetoric. He brought his analytical talent to the study of documents, establishing an important practice in historical source-analysis. Valla's privately-funded and published *Discourse on the Forgery of Constantine* (1439-40) questions the authenticity of the Donation of Constantine, a document which appeared to 'prove' that in the fourth century the Emperor Constantine had given the Bishop of Rome sovereign power over the city of Rome.

The Donation of Constantine *depicted by members of Raphael's workshop (1520-1524), in the Vatican's Sala di Costantino.*

Although Otto of Freising had expressed skepticism about the document's authenticity, he offered no systematic way to verify his doubts. Using philological techniques, Valla argued conclusively that vocabulary and idioms employed in the Donation came from much later than the document's putative origin. He also emphasised that, because no authentic document from the time of the Donation's putative origins referred to it, the document was a later creation, a forgery. It's important to remember, however, that Valla was in the service of the King of Aragon and Sicily, who was then at war with the pope. Valla's study of the Donation, which was the foundation of the Papacy's landed power, was therefore part of a propaganda campaign. (Anyone doubting the convincing nature of literary forgeries and their political nature should think about the so-called *Hitler Diaries* scandal of the 1980s.)

Valla's demonstration of forgery undermined a fundamental assumption about the nature of continuity. He had shown that contemporary Europe was not the inheritor of an unbroken intellectual continuity from the world of classical antiquity. There was something qualitatively different between the two periods, and these differences had been instantiated by sharp breaks in thinking. The time between these breaks also had their own character – this is what we now think of as periodization.

Obviously, this posed a serious challenge to the idea of temporal life on earth being governed by the salvation economy, coherent and contiguous blocks of time in between Christ's life on earth and his anticipated return at the end of time. Petrarch and Valla were genuine believers (Petrarch's *Secretum* was a dialogue with the long-dead St Augustine, in which he poured out his soul to Augustine), but their writing about time and documentary proof had changed the relationship between Christianity and history. Now it seemed more possible to look back on the achievements of antiquity without the concern that they had been pagans. Acknowledging the fundamental difference between the fifteenth century and antiquity meant that Renaissance scholars could examine clearly and emulate technically those writers of antiquity like Thucydides and Livy, without having to adopt their religious persuasions.

Lorenzo Valla's technical judgment about a single document had much wider ramifications for history-writing and contemporary politics. His 'conversation' with Petrarchan ideas formed a response to previous eras and their assumptions.

Think laterally

1. Can you think of another document which has caused one age to question the assumptions of a previous age? Explain how.

___

The Renaissance humanists who emerged in northern Italy's independent city-state republics read the works of historians from republican Rome, especially Livy, in the light of contemporary internal conflict after the French invasion of Italy in 1494. Two Florentine scholars broke radically with the conventional framework of mediaeval history writing. The diplomat (*overleaf*) Niccolo Machiavelli's *The Prince* and *Commentaries* (on Livy's *History of Rome*) and his preface to the *History of Florence* collectively explained Florence's weakening republican institutions as the result of the citizens' loss of *virtu*, or patriotic commitment. Machiavelli rejected the medieval habit of chronicling, which lacked both overall shape and writing elegance, and produced a logical and fluent narrative interested in cause and effect. He was, however, more interested in the political aspect of events, and his narrative therefore left out a great many things and focused unduly on others which he felt had political 'lessons' for readers.

Another diplomat, Francesco Giucciardini, sometimes described as Machiavelli's rival as a historian, also wrote a *History of Florence*, which focused on the period 1378-1509. His narrative was precise, his handling of sources insightful, and he balanced a good analysis of

character with an ability to understand the overall series of affairs in which the personalities arose. He also wrote an *History of Italy* about the political events from 1492-1534, arguing that the once-independent city states had been subordinated to Spain and France because aspiring rulers invariably sought to increase their power by weakening their rivals. His works were extremely popular, and by 1600 they had been translated into six other languages and were read by everyone from emperors to schoolboys.

The emerging Florentine analytical and pragmatic approach spread to both France and England. Claude Seyssel and Robert Gaguin rejected the use of legend and conventional morality and instead highlighted the recent successes of French kings in the Hundred Years War against England and against Burgundians. Both sought to show that French law was unique and had evolved separately from earlier Roman legal codes. Through the diplomatic activities of the Italian churchman Polydore Vergil, the Florentine tradition of history-writing spread to England. In 1525 Vergil published an edition of the 6th-century monk Gildas's *De Excidio et Conquestu Britanniae*, the first critical edition of a British historical text. He subjected the sources of English history, which had been both ridiculed and beloved by English historians, to serious criticism, and dismissed the foundational legends of Arthur. The work of Geoffrey of Monmouth, which had been authoritative because there was nothing as comprehensive to challenge it, was finally put to rest as a series of fascinating but baseless fables. Vergil continued Gildas' work at the invitation of Henry VII, completing *Anglica Historia* in 1512–13. It was not, however, published until 1534 because of the turbulent political climate.

Clarify

2. What are the key characteristics of the Florentine tradition of history-writing?

_____
_____
_____
_____
_____
_____

Other Peoples, Other Histories

Another impact of the Renaissance and the burgeoning Age of Exploration was that European scholars now had to account for newly-discovered peoples, often with their own traditions of recording and transmitting knowledge of the past. Perhaps the most important example of this is Bartolomé de las Casas, whose *A Short Account of the Destruction of the Indies* (1552, illustrated by Theodor de Bry, see *below*) and *Historia de Las Indias* (1561), chronicle the first decades of colonization of the West Indies in a critical way, describing the genocide and atrocities brought by Europeans against the indigenous peoples of the New World. Since many of the explorers were Spanish and Portuguese clerics from the Dominican and Jesuit orders, their commitment to the Christian conception of history was implicit, but they were also intellectual pragmatists who were interested in the new peoples for their own sake and recognized fundamentally different ways of thinking about time and its narrative record. Las Casas lived a long and eventful life, writing a vast output and placing his history-writing at the service of politics, particularly social justice. His work is a reminder that until relatively recently almost all historians have participated in public life. The fact that his *Historia de Las Indias* was not published for 314 years after its composition reflects the resistance to entrenched ideas about other peoples.

Although there were exceptions, such as Girolamo Benzoni's *History of the New World,* many of the documents that were published in the sixteenth century about the new peoples and places with which Europeans came into contact were accounts of personal adventure and novelty. They were written in a consciously self-dramatizing style and positioned the indigenous peoples of the 'new world' as little more than props or plot-devices which cemented the idea that Europe (and perhaps some parts of the Far East) had a legitimate sense of history and everywhere else had no consciousness of its own past. This idea is made admirably clear by the Italian Peter Martyr d'Anghiera, whose 1530 book *De Orbe Novo* was translated into English in 1555 as *The Decades of the newe worlde* by Richard

Eden. Eden combined it with several other works, including Gonzalo Oviedo's *Natural hystoria de las Indias* to make an extremely popular work which captures the way Europeans saw the people they came to treat so poorly:

> these simple gentiles lyvinge only after the lawe of nature, may well bee likened to a smoothe and bare table unpainted, or a white paper unwritten upon, upon the which yow may at the first paynte and wryte what yow lyste.

Think laterally

3. Suggest some effects of a clash between two different traditions of history-writing. Remember that this clash is taking place amid a colonizing context.

___

In Europe, the religious conflicts known as the Reformation affected history-writing - and every other aspect of life and thought. Martin Luther challenged basic church teachings and practices such as the doctrine of predestination, the selling of papal indulgences and the privileged position of clergy in the interpretation of scripture. Both sides in the Catholic-Protestant divide turned to the past to justify their theological and ecclesiastical stances. The resultant 'confessionalisation' – that is, a focus on formulating and expounding doctrinal orthodoxy rather than interpreting the significance of past events – of history lasted until well into the 20th century.

One group of Protestant historians made an important innovation which eventually became a convention of the discipline. The creators of the mid-16th century *Magdeburg Confessions* — a massive compilation of data about Catholic Church corruption – organised the materials in volumes each covering 100 years. This use of 'centuries' came to supplement earlier methods of sequencing the past into Ancient, Mediaeval or Modern eras or the reigns of dynasties, empires, or consuls. In this process, the Magdeburg Confessions created what Popkin calls

> a tenacious habit of thinking of centuries as periods with distinctive characteristics, a frame of mind that persists even when historians recognise that years ending in '00' rarely coincide with major historical transformations.

Think laterally

4. Name THREE other ways of grouping historical periods, and for each, suggest the effect of this method of grouping on the history-writing of that period.

___

Ancients vs Moderns

Writing in the first century AD, Livy had taken a gloomy attitude to the present, arguing that the past had been better before it gave in to an inevitable decline. This idea that 'the past was best' (and its corollary, 'the best was past') continued to come up as historians compared their own day to a largely imagined past. The Middle Ages viewed the ancient past as heroic though admittedly pagan, and the issue was formally debated in 1528 by the Dutch humanist Erasmus' dialogue, *Ciceronianus*, which claimed that academic Latin of the early modern period was vastly inferior to the Latin written by Cicero in the first century BC. Replies were written by Julius Caesar Scaliger and Etienne Dolet dismissing Erasmus' argument. Although these were largely linguistic arguments, the idea that antiquity (particularly the period of the late Roman Republic) was somehow finer, more elegant, more disciplined, and party to erudition, affected ways of writing history.

The 'Moderns' argued that what was new was better – a claim perpetually echoed until post-modernity's claim that nothing is new and everything is relative – and as proof pointed particularly to scientific inventions of the Early Modern Period. The printing press, instruments for measuring time and space, and perspectives on how the brain and mind worked suggested that, although the ancients had perfected the arts of their age, society should consciously endorse moving forward rather than nostalgic retrospection. In the late 17th century, the quarrel was best shown in the rivalry between the new science of the Royal Society and the now-venerable Aristotelian science enshrined in universities. Ironically to us, Isaac Newton counted himself an 'Ancient' and believed that religious figures of antiquity and biblical pre-history, such as Moses, had greater access to the truth of things that anything the modern world could shore up. As the Moderns prevailed and the value of studying the past was questioned, it became clear that history was crucial to identifying those factors which enable progress, and the obstacles which impede it.

The Print Revolution

The terms Renaissance, Reconaissance, and Reformation describe many of the changes which happened in a mere two hundred years. The 'Fourth R' - Revolution – reflects changes in technology. The movable type printing press developed by Johannes Gutenberg around 1460 brought about changes to historians' style and reading practices. More people could read more books; students could (just about) own their own copies of books; and historians could make criticisms of each other's work knowing that they were all discussing the same edition. The texts of Greek and Roman historians became more broadly available, as did historical documents – old laws and charters – so that historians then gained access to original sources in consistent forms, even if they had not been edited as rigorously as they are today.

Of course, the era of printing brought about its own problems – some of which were unique to historians, such as the authenticity of what was being printed, and the propriety of placing it in collections which, by being titled and categorized in one way, could give a false sense of the document's context. The speed with which opinion could be disseminated could be extremely dangerous; institutions like the Catholic Church developed a checking (and potentially censoring) system where books had to receive an *imprimatur* by an appropriate official such as a bishop. Books which did not receive this were placed on a list of prohibited books – the *Index Librorum Prohibitorum*, which was only abolished in 1966. Indeed, Catholic canon law still recommends that works on church history, doctrine, Scripture and morality should be submitted to a cleric like a bishop for approval. They will then consult an appropriate expert, and if the expert finds nothing objectionable in the text, it will be issued a *nihil obstat* ("nothing forbids"), then an *imprimatur* ("let it be printed"). Members of religious bodies need an *imprimi potest* ("it can be printed") from their order's superior to publish their work.

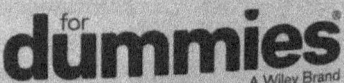

Catholicism for Dummies, *which still has a Nihil Obstat and Imprimatur*

Although there had been a daily bulletin of important news in republican Rome, it had been produced on stone or metal, and could not be possessed by the ordinary person. Printing technology facilitated a wider circulation of *avvisi*, or news-sheets (the forerunners of newspapers), about important current events. These could be bought by almost everyone; Italian states sold them for a *gazette*, a small coin, and they drastically altered the common man's sense of how quickly the world moved. Writers of such news-letters often also doubled as chroniclers and translators, blurring the line between 'current events' and 'history'.

As a way to regulate historical work in a period of greatly expanded intellectual effort, the academic journal and a rudimentary form of the peer review came into being. In the late 17th century, Pierre Bayle's *Nouvelles de la Republique de Lettres* reviewed newly published books. The *Nouvelles* came out monthly, then bi-monthly (after 1710), and was so popular that it had to be published in the more open-minded Amsterdam to avoid French censorship.

Amid these innovations in popular culture the 17th century witnessed the publication of four works that significantly influenced readers and their expectations. One was a sharply critical history of the Counter-Reformation by the Catholic Paolo Sarpi, which showed a capacity to separate personal religious beliefs from an intellectual evaluation of the governing institutions. A similar, but secular, example of intellectual distance can be found in Edward Hyde's *History of the Rebellion*. This was an account of the English Civil War from 1640-60 by a moderate Royalist participant that showed how strident royalism had resulted in the defeat and execution of Charles I, while the short-lived triumph of Parliament had resulted in the Restoration. Cardinal Bossuet's *Discourse and Universal History* (1681) defended the absolute power of Louis XIV using extensive documents from the Royal Archive, thus influencing other European rulers to create their own archives. Alexander Oexmelin's *History of the Buccaneers of America* (1678) (reworked many times, most recently in the popular film series *Pirates of the Caribbean*) was popular in several European languages, and in two continents, and was one of the first histories that focused on what we would today call 'non-state actors.'

Think laterally

A common way to establish a common historical bond with another person is to ask 'Where were you when...' (man walked on the Moon, Elvis died, JFK was shot, Princess Diana died, the Twin Towers were destroyed are all common ones).

5. Name and explain THREE effects of this historical consciousness in ordinary people.

_____
_____
_____
_____
_____
_____
_____

6. Do you think ordinary people before the Reformation would have had this historical consciousness? Explain your answer.

___

The Relegation of Memory

In this sudden influx of historical publications, care was not always taken before historians rushed into print. Indeed, so great were the number of factual errors, poorly-thought-out arguments, and spurious theories about the 'laws' by which human society operated that Pierre Bayle (*left*) published an encyclopaedia of ideas, the *Historical and Critical Dictionary*. In it he suggested that quite a lot of 'truth' was entirely subjective, and that many thinkers were guilty of being too proud to change their ideas when disproved. Like Abelard's 12th-century theological text *Sic et Non,* Bayle drew attention to the problems of contradiction by presenting the evidence of both sides of an argument. Unlike Abelard, however, he did not offer a method for resolving such contradictions but instead used their existence to argue for tolerance and an informed scepticism. Promoting a tolerant attitude to philosophical and religious differences, Bayle criticized many of the rationalists of the day, such as Descartes, Leibniz, Malebranche, and Hobbes. He disagreed strenuously with the idea that human reason can explain religious truths, and referred to the ancient Pyrrhonists, a type of Greek scepticism that advises us to maintain an intellectual modesty and suspended judgement in most non-practical matters. Bayle, like Giambattista Vico, is one of the 'heroes' of the early Enlightenment period, whose work was contentious in its own time, but which assisted the production of much more famous works and names. Although Vico's insight was later recognized in the nineteenth century, Pierre Bayle's contribution to organized, fair, and rigorous scholarship has never been properly acknowledged.

A resurgence of the academic scepticism from antiquity became apparent as some wondered if any kind of certainty about the past (or indeed, about knowledge itself) was even possible. Human scholarship could be very faulty. Divine inspiration was no longer credible, Baruch Spinoza had argued. So was there anything that we *could* be certain about? The answer came in the form of Rene Descartes' radically simple but far-reaching idea that we could be certain of our own existence, because we were thinking about it – an idea captured by the maxim *cogito sum ergo* (I think, therefore, I am).

Although Descartes (*left*) proposed an apparently solid way to be sure that we knew something, he was sceptical about the reliability and utility of other parts of the intellect, such as memory. In keeping with the 'present-ism' of his philosophical perspective, Descartes did not see how the past could contribute to the present or future except in a purely causal sense. If you wanted to know the best way to act, the evidence of previous events was irrelevant; only the application of principles of reason was any use in the current moment. He presented four arguments against the existence of history as a branch of knowledge. One was that, by studying the past the historian ends up unfamiliar with his own time – and perhaps useless to it. A second was that 'the events which [history] described never happened exactly as it described them.' A third was that, because the narratives are untrustworthy, they cannot help us to decide how to act in the present. The fourth objection was that historians distort the past by making it seem more splendid than it really was.

7. How would you refute these objections? Develop your own answers and then look at what the modern historian R.G. Collingwood said.

_____

_____

_____

_____

_____

_____

Francis Bacon, another philosopher who made contributions to epistemology, also considered the use and meaning of empirical evidence, but employed the concept of observation quite differently to Descartes. While Descartes saw the past and its products as irrelevant to questions about how to act in the present, Bacon thought that the continued existence of source-materials from the past *in* the present meant that their present relevance was obvious. In studying the sources, one could apply the principles of observation, hypothesis, and deduction just as one could to natural history and points of reason. He explicitly rejected the deductive method in favour of the inductive, and thus gave new urgency to the need for reliable, rigorous methods of source-handling and the evaluation of the narratives drawn from, and carried by, these sources. Bacon's influence encouraged Jean Mabillon (1632-1707), a Benedictine monk, to establish the study of documents, which we now call 'diplomatic'.

Mabillon accepted that apparently conclusive evidence might still be insufficient proof of a hypothesis because of the possibility of forgery. He produced a work which medievalists still refer to, the *De re diplomatica*, a handbook and primer of different medieval manuscript documents, scripts, signatures, seals and other important elements of physical and textual composition. At a time when collections of documents were beginning to be printed, Mabillon's work reminded the historian that acquaintance with the actual primary sources, not simply printed transcriptions of them, was absolutely necessary. They had to have a solid knowledge of the principles and context of manuscript construction, as well as a repertoire of manuscripts, hands, and codices with which they were intimately familiar.

Valla and Bayle's emphases on critical method coupled with Spinoza's rejection of scriptural authority encouraged an increasingly rigorous scepticism in the writing of history and the handling of historical sources. The resulting histories were written with a secular eye to the future, rather than conceptualising human experience as a story of progress towards a God-given end.

Clarify

8. Why do you think Mabillon's insistence on documents being studied together was impossible before the seventeenth century?

9. For your own understanding, write down the relationship between Bayle's, Spinoza's, and Descartes' ideas.

CONCEPT FOCUS 3: AUXILIARY SCIENCES

Transcribe this letter, observing all the capital letters, spelling mistakes, line breaks, and punctuation.

Braxton county Va   March the 14, 1853
Dear husband it is with mutch respect
That I embrace the present oppertunity to let
you now that me and the children are well at this
Time and to cincerly hope that these few lines
May reach and find you enjoying good health and
All the necessary comforts of camp life I received
a letter from you yesterday which gave me the gratest
Satisfaction to that you was still a live but it greives
me to think that it will be so long be fore we shall
be premitted to see each oter if ever the rest of
your frienets is all well as far as inow ihave ben
staying at your fathers for some time but am going
home if ican get enybody to stay with me ihavent
Ben at home since the first of febuary and havent
Seen one of them Luther says he wants you to fetch
him a penknife he says he would like to see his
Pappy he is a bad boy he swears yet litte vanycan
run just where he pleases he is as fat as a litte pig
I am by mi self to day and i fell lonesom iwish you
was here with me idont think that iwould
be very lonly iwant you to take good care of
your self and try and get home once more
    Give my best respects to clinton and the doctor
Tell them that there famlys are both well
    So I will have to bring my letter to a close by
Asking you to right evry schanel you hav
For it gives me the gratest satisfaction in the world
To hear from you so imust close

DE
RE DIPLOMATICA,
LIBER PRIMUS,

In quo veterum Inftrumentorum antiquitas, materia, & fcripturæ explicantur.

CAPUT PRIMUM.

I. *Operis utilitas.* II. *Occafio.* III. *Scopus.* IV. *Duo extrema vitanda.*

OVUM antiquariæ artis genus aggredior, in qua de veterum inftrumentorum ratione, formulis & auctoritate agitur. Præcipuam eis fidem, fi modò vera & genuina fuerint, tribuendam effe cenfent omnes, maximè quantum ad rei tranfactæ circumftantias & ad res chronologicas attinet, quæ nullo aliunde certiori teftimonio, quàm ejufmodi monumentis refciri & confirmari poffunt. Verùm iidem ipfi, qui hoc inftrumentorum genus probant, quædam in eis falfa, fufpecta, interpolata circumferri caufantur: & dum in iftis difcernendis hærent, etiam indubitatis fidem temere abrogant aliquando. At valde mirum effet, fi in tanta autographorum & exemplorum varietate, quæ ex tam longa annorum ferie, per tot diverfarum nationum manus ad nos tranfmiffa funt, adulterina aut vitiofa nulla reperirentur. Sed inquirendum, quàm latè pateat hoc malum, & fi qua tandem arte ipfi occurri poffit: ne rei litterariæ illa pars, quæ potiorem fibi auctoritatem meritò vindicat, vanis exceptionibus atque cenfuris impune violetur.

Quanta fit iftius artis utilitas ac neceffitas, nemo non videt: cùm non folùm ecclefiaftica & civilis hiftoria, fed maximè privatorum hominum, ecclefiarumque fortunæ plurimùm pendeant ex ejufmodi monumentis. Quam ob rem magnopere intereft ad antiquariam forenfemque difciplinam hæc tractatio: magnamque à re publica gratiam inierit, quifquis certas & accuratas tradiderit conditiones ac regulas, quibus inftrumenta legitima à fpuriis, certa & genuina ab incertis ac fufpectis fecernantur. Verùm ad id argumentum pro dignitate tractandum opus effet in primis eruditione non vulgari, tum multo veterum chartarum atque archivorum ufu, quibus fumma

A

VILLE DE LYON
Biblioth. du Palais des Arts

The 1759 edition of Mabillon's De re diplomatica, *showing the typesetting of the beautiful and extremely clear italic script developed during the Italian Renaissance, which was derived from the Carolingian miniscule hand of the 8th century. The mis-en-page of this book, which was meant to be used like a primer, was elegant, rational, and extremely easy to use.*

History as cycles

Contemporary to the Ancients vs Moderns debate was the Italian philosopher Giambattista Vico (*left,* 1668-1744), whose work really only came to be appreciated in the twentieth century. Vico distinguished between two types of knowledge, and the degrees and kinds of certainty that we can achieve from them. On the one hand, knowledge of the natural world was derived from objective observation and hypothesis. On the other, knowledge of the human world came from instigation, participation, and subjective recollection. Because history is a purely human thing (that is, a conception of the human past and our actions in it), we can 'know' things about history – and in ways – that we cannot know things about the natural world, because we did not make it.

Vico further contributed a tripartite and cyclical theory of history: a divine age, in which people saw the hand of divine agents in events; a heroic age, in which the prime movers were cultural elites (who often claimed to have divine origin); and a secular age in which more or less rational human government was ascendant. Although he generally believed in the concept of progress, he saw this as part of a larger cycle of change and renewal – *corso i ricorso*. This was less troubling than Christianity's view of a headlong plunge towards the End of Days, but it also foresaw the inevitable decline of a society which was rational and secular, before being renewed in the 'divine' age. Like Ibn Khaldun, Vico contributed a list of errors into which historians are likely to fall. They included: the belief that antiquity was more magnificent than it really was; the prejudice in favour of one's own nation and people; the belief that historically interesting people were just like historians, reflective theorists and intellectuals, when they usually weren't; the idea that two nations with similar institutions were connected causally; and the belief that those temporally closest to the events knew the most about it. Many of these errors can be explained by the natural vanity of praising what is familiar or similar to ourselves, and the natural laziness of thinking that 'closest is truest'.

Vico balanced these criticisms with an insightful and common-sensical understanding of what we *could* gain from historical information, if we were prepared to work for it. Historical knowledge was not something that you simply imbibed passively from a teacher; students of history had to think, evaluate, synthesise, and interpret, putting together a narrative for themselves. They had to understand the language of the people they studied, in a profound way – it wasn't simply enough to learn Latin. You had to know how Latin-users saw their language, in the same way that English learners who learn the language solely from a textbook will have an awkward, partial, and probably false idea of what is meant in real-world texts. Similarly, the use of mythology and tradition had to be maturely done: myths and habits were often the expressions of more deeply-rooted convictions, and were not to be taken at face value. To test our understanding, he argued, we had to remember that societies *developed* in the same way that people do. We move towards more abstract ways of expressing complex beliefs – Vico suggested that to understand primitive cultures we should look at those in primitive stages of our own culture, such as children. He was, essentially, formulating developmental psychology some two centuries before it appeared as a discipline, yet Vico's insight and common sense was not recognized for at least two generations after his death.

Think laterally

10. In this period, the concept of 'progress' arose. What do you understand by that? Give as detailed an explanation as possible.

Some people believe that the concept of progress is central to a secular view of History.

11. What problems can you identify with the idea of 'progress' for theocentric historians?

Reading task 3

Read the following passages.

Niccolo Machiavelli, Florentine Histories

The people who inhabit the northern parts beyond the Rhine and the Danube, living in a healthy and prolific region, frequently increase to such vast multitudes that part of them are compelled to abandon their native soil, and seek a habitation in other countries. The method adopted, when one of these provinces had to be relieved of its superabundant population, was to divide into three parts, each containing an equal number of nobles and of people, of rich and of poor. The third upon whom the lot fell, then went in search of new abodes, leaving the remaining two-thirds in possession of their native country.

These migrating masses destroyed the Roman empire by the facilities for settlement which the country offered when the emperors abandoned Rome, the ancient seat of their dominion, and fixed their residence at Constantinople; for by this step they exposed the western empire to the rapine of both their ministers and their enemies, the remoteness of their position preventing them either from seeing or providing for its necessities. To suffer the overthrow of such an extensive empire, established by the blood of so many brave and virtuous men, showed no less folly in the princes themselves than infidelity in their ministers; for not one irruption alone, but many, contributed to its ruin; and these barbarians exhibited much ability and perseverance in accomplishing their object.

Bartolome de las Casas' *History of the Indies*.

The Spaniards entered the province of Camaguey, which is large and densely populated . . . and when they reached the villages, the inhabitants had prepared as well as they could cassava bread from their food; what they called *guaminiquinajes* from their hunting; and also fish, if they had caught any.

Immediately upon arriving at a village, the cleric Casas would have all the little children band together; taking two or three Spaniards to help him, along with some sagacious Indians of this island of Hispaniola, whom he had brought with him, and a certain servant of his, he would baptize the children he found in the village. He did this throughout the island . . . and there were many for whom God provided holy baptism because He had predestined them to glory. God provided it at a fitting time, for none or almost none of those children remained alive after a few months....

When the Spaniards arrived at a village and found the Indians at peace in their houses, they did not fail to injure and scandalize them. Not content with what the Indians freely gave, they took their wretched subsistence from them, and some, going further, chased after their wives and daughters, for this is and always has been the Spaniards' common custom in these Indies. Because of this and at the urging of the said father, Captain Narvaez ordered that after the father had separated all the inhabitants of the village in half the houses, leaving the other half empty for the Spaniards' lodging, no one should dare go to the Indians' section. For this purpose, the father would go ahead with three or four men and reach a village early; by the time the Spaniards came, he had already gathered the Indians in one part and cleared the other.

Thus, because the Indians saw that the father did things for them, defending and comforting them, and also baptizing their children, in which affairs he seemed to have more command and authority than others, he received much respect and credit throughout the island among the Indians. Further, they honored him as they did their priests, magicians, prophets, or physicians, who were all one and the same.

Because of this ... it became unnecessary to go ahead of the Spaniards. He had only to send an Indian with an old piece of paper on a stick, informing them through the messenger that those letters said thus and so. That is, that they should all be calm, that no one should absent himself because he would do them no harm, that they should have food prepared for the Christians and their children ready for baptism, or that they should gather in one part of the village, and anything else that it seemed good to counsel them—and that if they did not carry these things out, the father would be angry, which was the greatest threat that could be sent them...

1. How do the two historians differ in their attitude to historical content?

2. Suggest the purpose of each history: you might consider the intended audience, and the language in which the work was originally written.

ISBN 9780645591422

Chapter revision statement

Write a list of the key points from this chapter.

_____
_____
_____
_____
_____
_____
_____
_____
_____
_____

Use the list to write a short statement about important features in the discipline of History during the period studied in this chapter.

_____
_____
_____
_____
_____
_____
_____
_____
_____

Notes

_____
_____
_____
_____
_____
_____
_____
_____

Chapter 4: Enlightenment?

Voltaire, Hume, and Macaulay, three of the most prolific writers of the Enlightenment

The acutely critical perspective of the Enlightenment was only interesting to readers if it was conveyed in an inspiring narrative. This inspiring prose often included 'bold generalisations' about periods and societies, although now historians were prepared to include the societies and peoples outside Europe. The source-critical approach of Mabillon, and the polemical tone of Valla were not palatable to an ever-increasing reading public. To meet the demands of an audience who had the money to buy books but not necessarily much literary taste, writers (including historians), developed new text-types in which historical writing was often blended with other literary forms.

The best exponent of the 'blended style' is Voltaire (François-Marie Arouet), who wrote historical plays, essays, poetry and scientific analysis, as well as 'pure' history. Yet even his historical writing took the slightly different approach of focusing on an 'age', or the spirit of a period. His *Age of Louis XIV* (1751) chronicled not only the wars and political events of the Sun King, but the cultural changes and social ideals in the first modern attempt at integrated history. He asserted in a Tacitean manner that

> we shall confine ourselves to that which deserves the attention of all time, which paints the spirits in the customs of men, which may serve for instruction and to counsel the love of virtue, of the arts and the Fatherland.

Ironically, although Voltaire was fiercely anti-clerical (and his writing was censored mercilessly by the Church), it was through the Church's agency, and particularly that of the Jesuit order, that Voltaire learned about non-Christian nations and cultures. His *Essay on the Customs and Spirits of the Nations* (1756) also aimed to 'paint the spirits in the customs of men', but by taking an extremely broad scope Voltaire showed two things. First, that the customs of other peoples were of equal scholarly interest as those of European Christians, and second, that historical writing should therefore treat their histories equally. While Voltaire's work had limited impact on the development of historiography in the long term, it was popular, and his revelation that current prejudices often produced a distorted image of the past reminded readers that well-written history created an important sense of critical perspective. He was not, however, above applying his own bias, and in a way that would come to be emulated in fiction by Dickens and the nineteenth-century satirical novelists, Voltaire 'sat in judgement on each person and event and passed sentence on them.'

The (financial) power of a good historical narrative

Five British writers applied the approach of critical survey and broad perspective in their own writing.

The Scottish philosopher David Hume is famous for the area of study that we now call psychology but which was known to the 18th century as natural science. Like Aristotle before him and Kant afterwards, Hume proposed a theory of human knowledge which was firmly rooted in our experience of the physical world. He made an important contribution to the philosophy of history in his suggestion that we are all immersed in the 'constant conjunction' of events which significantly limits what we can know. We do not see one event linking to the next as a series of discrete units, because we experience history as a seamless flow. This makes it particularly difficult to judge what we will do in the future, and also to recollect the causes and effects of things in the past which we have experienced as a totality.

Hume's six-volume *History of England* (1759-61) benefitted from his position as a relative outsider. As a Scot, he could apply an objectivity to the English tradition which English historians had lacked. Thus his 'relatively positive portrayal of the Stuart kings' acknowledged that reform had been necessary, while deploring the violence with which this had been achieved. It outraged the Whig political party, which saw itself as the descendants of the Civil War parliamentarians who had executed Charles I. This is perhaps evidence that the seamless flow of experience led to inherited biases.

One such Whig historian was Catharine Macaulay, whose eight-volume *History of England from the Accession of James I to the Revolution* (1763-83) sought to remind British people that the liberties which they enjoyed had been fought for against

> the formidable pretensions of the Stewart family, and set up the banners of liberty against a tyranny which had been established for a series of more than one hundred and fifty years.

She justified the regicide but was critical of Cromwell and the Glorious Revolution. The love-hate relationship between Macauley, sections of the Whig party, and contemporary *literati* is evidence that most 18th-century writing cannot be separated from social and political clubs and groups which are an area of study in their own right.

The Scottish historian and economic theorist Adam Ferguson's *Essay on the History of Civil Society* (1782) recalled Vico's paradigm of history as a three-stage cycle. Ferguson's model was one of increasing economic complexity, from the pastoral to the manufacturing, and speculated about the consequences (not entirely positive) of the development of what we now call a market economy. The book was acclaimed and taught at the University of Moscow – ironically, since its section on the division of labour influenced Karl Marx.

Like Hume, William Robertson's *History of the Reign of Charles V* (1769) and *History of America* (1777) gained both recognition and some popularity, perhaps because it threw light on the revolution in Britain's North American colonies. Unlike the other British historians of this period, Robertson was a cleric, becoming chaplain of Stirling Castle and one of the King's Chaplains in Scotland.

As Jeremy Popkin notes, what is important historiographically about these historians is that they all did well financially from their extremely intensive, multi-volume, labours. Their financial successes showed that historians could indeed make a living from their skills, as long as they could compose a narrative which met the public's taste which was for long-form, epic-scope, nation-focused, dense writing.

The undoubted champion of this style of writing was Edward Gibbon (*above*), whose massive *Decline and Fall of the Roman Empire* (1776-1789) outstripped all others and has remained an enduring historical and literary classic. Gibbon's success can be explained not only by the massive scope of his writing but also for his accompanying *Memoirs* (1796). As one of the first modern British autobiographies his memoirs act as a parallel narrative to the *Decline and Fall*, and tell the story of how he developed his project, rather like Herodotus' account of his travels:

> To methodise the form, and to collect the substance of my Roman decay… were my old and familiar companions. …I investigated, with my pen almost always in my hand, the original records, both in Greek and Latin…The subsidiary rays of medals and inscriptions of geography and chronology were thrown on their proper objects…[to] fix and arrange within my reach the loose and scattered atoms of historical information… At the outset all was dark and doubtful: even the title of the work…and I was often tempted to caste away the labour of seven years… Many experiments were made before I could hit the middle tone between a dull chronicle and a rhetorical declamation… my pride was soon humbled, and a sober melancholy was spread over my mind, by the idea that I had taken an everlasting leave of an old and agreeable companion, and that whatever might be the future of my History, the life of the historian must be short and precarious.

Gibbon's underlying theme in this *magnum opus* was an anti-clerical one: Christianity's values were antithetical to those of the Roman Empire's and they eventually eroded the *virilitas*, *auctoritas*, and *culti* upon which the Empire had been built. Where Voltaire smacked of outright anti-clericalism, Gibbon played to an audience increasingly aware of how little religious authority influenced contemporary society. Although modern scholarship has rendered much of Gibbon's thesis redundant, his literary masterpiece remains an outstanding expression of Enlightenment thought. Like Hume, Gibbon enjoyed considerable commercial success, and his work remains in popular print and readership to this day.

In France, the Baron de Montesquieu (*above left*) wrote *Spirit of Laws (1748),* an attempt at a philosophy of history, in which the concept of causation was taken up more intensely than it had been since Polybius. Montesquieu pointed out that there was often a general cause behind significant events like the loss of a battle, and this general cause or spirit of the time was a more potent force than any action of individual genius. Frequently the spirit of the time was informed by changes in the natural world such as climate or geography, to which humans were forced to accommodate themselves. The way they accommodated such large-scale changes resulted in customs, and custom was always the best law, Montesquieu argued, in comparison with practises imposed by the ideals of a few. Montesquieu thus positioned man as a part of nature rather than separate from it, or the 'master' of it. This was a significant check to the Judeo-Christian idea of 'dominion' in which human beings had the right and duty to subordinate nature to themselves.

Also working from a political perspective was the Marquis de Condorcet's *Sketch for a Historical Picture of the Progress of the Human Mind* (1794), written in the midst of the French Revolution. Condorcet (*above right*) took this 'psychological model' and made even more prominent the idea of progress in the development of the human being. Condorcet's contribution is perhaps to make change intrinsic, and consciousness of change prominent, in the construction of a historical narrative. It is particularly ironic that Condorcet wrote this work in hiding from the Republicans, despite his ardent support of the Republican ideals.

Clarify

1. Gibbon characterises his topic as an 'old and agreeable companion'. Suggest the effect of working on a single topic for most of your life.

___

Think laterally

The Enlightenment was the great age of satire, perhaps because many intellectuals recognized the gap between society's new reach and aspirations, and the often-disappointing reality which transpired.

2. Do you think History can be satirical; if so, why and with what effect?

___

3. Condorcet eventually died in prison after hiding from the Revolutionaries, despite having championed their cause. What effect does this knowledge have on your evaluation of his ideas?

___

4. Read about either Montesquieu or Condorcet. What contributions did they make to history – and many other disciplines?

___

CONCEPT FOCUS 4: STYLE

Enlightenment history is frequently polemical. The men and women who wrote it did not treat the periods or personalities about which they wrote as remote or neutral. The topics they chose were often deeply entwined with the historian's own life, experiences, and beliefs. This accounts for the passionate and sometimes even propagandistic approach to their material.

Edward Gibbon was sixteen when he converted to Catholicism and was baptised into the Church. He was expelled from university, because at the time Oxford did not educate Catholics, and he was likewise unable to hold any civil job. His father was mortified by his son's conversion and sent him to Switzerland to be 're-educated' by a Calvinist. The entire experience changed Gibbon's attitude to religion entirely: he became an agnostic and remained skeptical about religion generally.

Although Gibbon's attribution of the Roman Empire's decline to Christianity's enfeebling influence has been challenged, the polemical style in which he writes has always been admired. As you read this passage (and it helps to read it aloud), consider the effect on the reader's perception of the argument of: adjectives and adverbs; abstract nouns; the use of nominalization; the passive voice; balanced sentences; the cumulative effect of many clauses, and the movement from generalizations to remarks about Gibbon's own time:

> As the happiness of a future life is the great object of religion, we may hear, without surprise or scandal, that the introduction, or at least the abuse, of Christianity had some influence on the decline and fall of the Roman empire. The clergy successfully preached the doctrines of patience and pusillanimity; the active virtues of society were discouraged; and the last remains of the military spirit were buried in the cloister; a large portion of public and private wealth was consecrated to the specious demands of charity and devotion; and the soldiers' pay was lavished on the useless multitudes of both sexes, who could only plead the merits of abstinence and chastity. Faith, zeal, curiosity, and the more earthly passions of malice and ambition kindled the flame of theological discord; the church, and even the state, were distracted by religious factions, whose conflicts were sometimes bloody, and always implacable; the attention of the emperors was diverted from camps to synods; the Roman world was oppressed by a new species of tyranny; and the persecuted sects became the secret enemies of their country. Yet party-spirit, however pernicious or absurd, is a principle of union as well as of dissension. The bishops, from eighteen hundred pulpits, inculcated the duty of passive obedience to a lawful and orthodox sovereign; their frequent assemblies, and perpetual correspondence, maintained the communion of distant churches: and the benevolent temper of the gospel was strengthened, though confined, by the spiritual alliance of the Catholics. The sacred indolence of the monks was devoutly embraced by a servile and effeminate age; but, if superstition had not afforded a decent retreat, the same vices would have tempted the unworthy Romans to desert, from baser motives, the standard of the republic. Religious precepts are easily obeyed, which indulge and sanctify the natural inclinations of their votaries; but the pure and genuine influence of Christianity may be traced in its beneficial, though imperfect, effects on the Barbarian proselytes of the North. If the decline of the Roman empire was hastened by the conversion of Constantine, his victorious religion broke the violence of the fall, and mollified the ferocious temper of the conquerors.

> This awful revolution may be usefully applied to the instruction of the present age. It is the duty of a patriot to prefer and promote the exclusive interest and glory of his native country; but a philosopher may be permitted to enlarge his views, and to consider Europe as one great republic, whose various inhabitants have attained almost the same level of politeness and cultivation. The balance of power will continue to fluctuate, and the prosperity of our own or the neighbouring kingdoms may be alternately exalted or depressed; but these partial events cannot essentially injure our general state of happiness, the system of arts, and laws, and manners, which so advantageously distinguish, above the rest of mankind, the Europeans and their colonies. The savage nations of the globe are the common enemies of civilized society; and we may inquire with anxious curiosity, whether Europe is still threatened with a repetition of those calamities which formerly oppressed the arms and institutions of Rome. Perhaps the same reflections will illustrate the fall of that mighty empire, and explain the probable causes of our actual security.

Not all historians write in a polemical style, but the relationship between style, purpose, and material is important in historiography because it reveals how the writer understands their audience and their own task. It is also one of the reasons why having a good grasp of different languages is valuable, since it is often difficult to judge style in translation.

Look at this passage from Winston Churchill's account of a debate about Britain's readiness for war in the 1930s. Consider how the elements of Churchill's style reflect aspects of his own biography and contribute to his purpose and material:

> Although the House listened to me with close attention, I felt a sensation of despair. To be so entirely convinced and vindicated in a matter of life and death to one's country, and not to be able to make Parliament and the nation heed the warning, or bow to the proof by taking action, was an experience most painful. I went on:
>
> "I confess that words fail me. In the year 1708 Mr. Secretary St. John, by a calculated Ministerial indiscretion, revealed to the House the fact that the Battle of Almanza had been lost in the previous summer because only 8,000 English troops were actually in Spain out of the 29,000 that had been voted by the House of Commons for this service.... the House sat in silence for half an hour, no Member caring to speak or wishing to make a comment upon so staggering an announcement. And yet how incomparably small that event was to what we have now to face...."
>
> There lay in my memory at this time some lines from an unknown writer about a railway accident. I had learnt them from a volume of Punch cartoons which I used to pore over when I was eight or nine years old at school at Brighton.
>
> > Who is in charge of the clattering train?
> > The axles creak and the couplings strain,
> > And the pace is hot, and the points are near,
> > And Sleep has deadened the driver's ear;
> > And the signals flash through the night in vain,
> > For Death is in charge of the clattering train.
>
> However, I did not repeat them.

Universal progress or different standards?

Jean-Pierre Houël, *The Storming of the Bastille*

As you have seen in the Concept Focus on Grand Narratives, historians often shape their material around a narrative which holds particular meaning and relevance to them. One of the most enduring narratives has been that of 'Progress'. Herbert Butterfield has described the narrative of progress as the idea 'which made it possible to give shape and structure to the course of ages. In a way it contributed a meaning to history'. Unlike the histories written from a religious perspective, the idea of a progress provided a meaning which referred to humans' own ideas of themselves rather than the idea of a providential or divine plan. It could also be measured, which justified the period's interest in mathematics, particularly statistics, and involved longitudinal surveys across sometimes very large spans of time indeed.

The trouble with the concept of progress is the implication that everyone is measured by the same yardstick. On the one hand, the 'Revolutionary School' rejected any reference – and certainly deference – to the past, and sought to tell the story of how 'modern' nation states, founded on rational ideals of equality and secularism, improved the quality of life for every citizen. They distinguished citizens from subjects, who merely existed to increase the possessions of a small group of nobles or clergy. The revolutions in America and France showed that it was possible to establish new nations on this basis, and Napoleon's conquests justified these nations militarily, by showing that modern republics could produce commanders as great as Alexander and Julius Caesar. Historians told the story of peoples, rather than individuals, emphasising the need to spread these revolutionary values across the 'civilized' world.

Such revolutions were bloody and became bloodier the longer they went on and the greater the divisions grew between revolutionary leaders. Robespierre and the Committee of Public Safety handed out 16,594 death sentences within a year, mostly to the middle-class people who would form the bulk of the Republic's bureaucracy. Other nations watched with horror as the revolution turned upon itself. Some, such as the Whig MP Edmund Burke, wrote about the instructional value of the past, and the revolutionaries' errors in ignoring this. His *Reflections on the Revolution in France* (1790) argued strongly in favour of drawing on experience rather than pure reason alone, and memorably defined a nation as a 'partnership not only between those who are living, but between those who are living, those who are dead and those who are to be born.' Revolutionary historians used one set of values – the French 'liberty, equality, and fraternity', or the American 'life, liberty, and the pursuit of happiness' (as well as unity and public virtue) – and judged other nations on the basis of their progress towards these ideals. In reality, though, the capacity to embed these ideals in daily life in a way that did not hinder economic health or material prosperity was the yardstick by which the success or failure of revolutions was – and still is – measured.

Romanticism and German *Volkische Geschefte*

This progress-oriented attitude to history, however, met a critical response in Germany, where the study of history had become a university speciality when the newly-founded University of Gottingen appointed the historian and statistician August Ludwig von Schlozer (*left*) as professor in 1734. Schlozer took a very broad view of national history, arguing that it was the study of government, cultural, and religious life, combined with statistics, politics, and geography. 'History,' he said, 'is statistics in motion. Statistics is stationary history.'

Unsurprisingly for a historian whose speciality was a quantifiable study of all aspects of a nation, Schlozer did not support the rather nebulous concept of 'progress' and its unqualified application to all nations. Other German writers at the time also argued that it was impossible and inappropriate to compare different nations, all with their own characters, mores and values, against some poorly-defined and externally-imposed measuring stick. Each nation should be judged only on its own terms, he said, since 'Each nationality contains its centre of happiness within itself, as a bullet the centre of gravity.'

This idea, so benign in its initial appearance, was given a sinister and careless form by the Romantic Johann Gottfried von Herder (*above right* 1744-1803). Rejecting the rationalism of the Enlightenment in favour of a Romanticism which prized emotion and spontaneity, Herder combined several ideas in a spirit of academic carelessness which R.G. Collingwood has said led straight to the Nazi marriage laws.

Herder's two massive books: *One More Philosophy of History* (1774) and *Ideas for the Philosophy of the History of Mankind* (1784-91) are primarily philosophical and use historical examples to support the argument rather than vice versa. The ideas which he combined in these two books included: a concept of cultural evolution; a fascination with race as the

foundation of differences between groups of people; the insistence that the culture of a people is best demonstrated by the common people rather than the upper classes or intelligentsia, and the idea of a historical 'mode' of existence as the arbiter between 'upper' and 'lower' races.

Herder argued that each race is shaped by its environment and will consequently develop its own ideas of the good and ideal life. However, the difference between peoples is not simply neutral but hierarchical, in virtue of how they relate to history and change. Alone of all peoples on Earth, the European has developed over time to higher and better forms of itself, and is thus the only genuinely 'historical' race. Almost the only idea which the twenty-first century might find palatable in Herder's unscientific admixture of racism and sentiment is the appreciation of the Middle Ages, which had been relegated during the Enlightenment as a savage and backward time.

The Romanticist historians, in R.G. Collingwood's opinion, widened the scope of historical study with their interest in the mysterious and exotic cultures of the East, and by their conception of history as a totality – past ages were all equally worthy of respect and interest, both for their own sake, and because they led to the present. Even Herder contributed a supremely valuable idea, which was that things must be judged by the standards of their own place and time, and that standing outside a different historical context and applying foreign judgments was meaningless. It was, therefore, extremely unfortunate that he chose to stand outside it all and apply hierarchies of superiority.

Think laterally

Measuring the features of a people or group according to its own standards, or its own understanding of itself, was clearly not what happened in Australia (and other colonies) when Europeans encountered the indigenous peoples.

5. Give an example of how this happened.

___

___

___

___

6. Is it possible to be truly 'relative' in writing a history of a people, or is it intrinsically opposed to the project of History? Explain your thoughts.

___

___

___

Think laterally

Our need to explain what things 'mean' is evident in the tenor of much internet content which pops up when something happens: 'What does it mean that Congress has found Trump to be a lunatic?' or 'What does it mean that water has been found on Mars?'

7. Do we really want to know what these 'mean' (if anything)? Or is there some other reason that the question is continually posed by a small number of public voices?

Think laterally

8. How do you define a nation? Does your definition have a historical dimension? What other political institutions (formal or informal) have a historical dimension?

Remember, you may have to define clearly what you mean by politics – so high schools might be a political institution.

The insistence on being measured by standards germane to the material, rather than the ideals of other countries and cultures, was particularly important to Germany, which was still a confederation of principalities, duchies, and small kingdoms, all with their own fiercely individual character. But it was also a perspective which British historians recognized. This nascent commonality of views in Britain and Germany developed more fully in the nineteenth century in opposition to the Francophone world, providing the Western historical tradition with two very different schools of thought.

In conclusion then, the seventeenth and eighteenth centuries were highly influential in the development of history-writing, separating history from the dominant religious framework of the Middle Ages and enabling writers to tell a more autonomous story of the human past. The rediscovery of ancient writers inspired authors, while the development of source-critical methods helped to clarify what constitutes historical truth. More than this, the printing press created new audiences as historians defended the value of their disciplined approach to the past and justified it as contributing to the construction of a better human future. Notwithstanding these apparently modern features, however, history writing at the end of the eighteenth century was not yet the activity we recognise today.

Clarify

9. For your own understanding, briefly summarize the differences between the Germanic and French schools of historical thought.

___

Extended response

That the past is always viewed through the lens of the present may seem to be obvious, but if we accept this suggestion, it means that stories of the past are always changing: that is, our present-day values and attitudes inform how we look back and review what has gone before. Moreover, the questions we put to the past are invariably shaped by our present.

Giselle Byrnes

10. Considering the historiographers you've read about, do you think this statement is true? What have you learned so far that makes you think so (or not)?

Don't worry too much about structure in your answer, just write your thoughts down. (Hint: A good way to get started is to paraphrase Byrnes' point to make sure you really understand.)

___

ISBN 9780645591422

Reading task 4

Read the following passage, from Hume's *History of England*. It comes from the end of the reign of Charles I, who was executed at the end of the Second English Civil War by the parliament, which governed England during the period of the Commonwealth, 1649-1660.

The height of all iniquity and fanatical extravagance yet remained—the public trial and execution of their sovereign. To this period was every measure precipitated by the zealous Independents. The parliamentary leaders of that party had intended, that the army themselves should execute that daring enterprise; and they deemed so irregular and lawless a deed best fitted to such irregular and lawless instruments. But the generals were too wise to load themselves singly with the infamy which, they knew, must attend an action so shocking to the general sentiments of mankind. The parliament, they were resolved, should share with them the reproach of a measure which was thought requisite for the advancement of their common ends of safety and ambition. In the house of commons, therefore, a committee was appointed to bring in a charge against the king. On their report a vote passed, declaring it treason in a king to levy war against his parliament, and appointing a high court of justice to try Charles for this new-invented treason. This vote was sent up to the house of peers.

The house of peers, during the civil wars, had all along been of small account; but it had lately, since the king's fall, become totally contemptible; and very few members would submit to the mortification of attending it. It happened that day to be fuller than usual, and they were assembled to the number of sixteen. Without one dissenting voice, and almost without deliberation, they instantly rejected the vote of the lower house, and adjourned themselves for ten days, hoping that this delay would be able to retard the furious career of the commons.

The commons were not to be stopped by so small an obstacle. Having first established a principle which is noble in itself, and seems specious, but is belied by all history and experience, "that the people are the origin of all just power;" they next declared, that the commons of England, assembled in parliament, being chosen by the people, and representing them, are the supreme authority of the nation, and that whatever is enacted and declared to be law by the commons, hath the force of law, without the consent of king or house of peers. The ordinance for the trial of Charles Stuart, king of England, (so they called him,) was again read, and unanimously assented to.

In proportion to the enormity of the violences and usurpations, were augmented the pretences of sanctity, among those regicides. "Should any one have voluntarily proposed," said Cromwell in the house, "to bring the king to punishment, I should have regarded him as the greatest traitor; but since Providence and necessity have cast us upon it, I will pray to God for a blessing on your counsels; though I am not prepared to give you any advice on this important occasion. Even I myself," subjoined he, "when I was lately offering up petitions for his majesty's restoration, felt my tongue cleave to the roof of my mouth, and considered this preternatural movement as the answer which Heaven, having rejected the king, had sent to my supplications."

A woman of Hertfordshire, illuminated by prophetical visions, desired admittance into the military council, and communicated to the officers a revelation, which assured them that their measures were consecrated from above, and ratified by a heavenly sanction. This intelligence gave them great comfort, and much confirmed them in their present resolutions.

Colonel Harrison, the son of a butcher, and the most furious enthusiast in the army, was sent with a strong party to conduct the king to London. At Windsor, Hamilton, who was there detained a prisoner, was admitted into the king's presence: and falling on his knees, passionately exclaimed, "My dear master!"—"I have indeed been so to you," replied Charles, embracing him. No further intercourse was allowed between them, The king was instantly hurried away. Hamilton long followed him with his eyes all suffused in tears, and prognosticated, that in this short salutation, he had given the last adieu to his sovereign and his friend.

1. Where are Hume's values evident – and what are these values?

2. At the time Hume was writing the separate nations of Scotland, England and Wales, (and at that time all of Ireland, not only the part remaining in the Union) had become the United Kingdom of Great Britain. Great Britain was enjoying military success in the Seven Years' War, a European conflict which strove to determine which nation would emerge as the leading colonial power. How does the tenor of Hume's own time affect his representation of England's past in the narrative?

3. Do you find Hume's style interesting to read? Give a personal reaction to the passage.

Chapter revision statement

Write a list of the key points from this chapter.

_____
_____
_____
_____
_____
_____
_____
_____
_____
_____

Use the list to write a short statement about important features in the discipline of History during the period studied in this chapter.

_____
_____
_____
_____
_____
_____
_____

Notes

_____
_____
_____
_____
_____
_____
_____

Chapter 5: The Academy and History

In the nineteenth century history secured its place in both European thought and in universities. Several German universities instituted a department of history, but it was in the philosophy departments that the most significant ideas about unifying and distinguishing features of the past were developed. Georg Hegel (*left*) was one of the leading figures of German Idealist philosophy, and his ideas about the progress of history as a series of oppositions and resolutions (known as 'Hegelian dialectic' and composed of a thesis, antithesis, and synthesis) continues to influence many fields of thought. For Hegel, the dialectical progression of ideas throughout history was a movement towards the 'absolute spirit' or human freedom. Indeed, since his was a purely idealistic paradigm, he maintained that all history *was* the history of human thought. Although historians should work with documentary evidence, they must look *through* or *within* those sources to find the thought or spirit behind them.

What Hegel meant by 'absolute spirit' or absolute freedom is at times very unclear in his vast *The Philosophy of History*, a series of lectures delivered in 1822-23. He took different ideas from other Idealists – Kant, Schiller, Schelling, Herder, and Fichte – but his thought is concerned with human control in self-and-world relations (a theme which is raised and again in German thought, politics, and culture). Absolute freedom is absolute self-knowledge, a specifically human type of reason which is the underlying force of all external events. This freedom is implemented in a thoroughly rational and moral reasoning, which in turn explains the process of opposition and accommodation or compromise which we call dialectic. Every idea (thesis) potentially contains in itself its opposite, and the two struggle with each other, exchanging parts and compromising, until a synthesis of the two is reached. The nature of the dialectical struggle informed the *zeitgeist* or spirit of the time, which was leveraged by exceptional people to cause changes that brough society closer to the absolute freedom. Its outward expression can be found in social relationships which Hegel believed had reached their zenith in the constitutional monarchies of his own day. History thus culminated in the present – specifically, Hegel's present – not in the future.

Unsurprisingly, this provoked strong reactions: Schopenhauer called the whole Hegelian machine 'a monument of German stupidity', and Croce argued that Hegel had confused opposition and distinction: things were not antithetical, but merely different. Other people disliked the idea that 'absolute freedom' had already been reached in the constitutional monarchies of Europe, calling it a lazy conservatism. Perhaps the most telling evaluation of Hegel's ideas can be seen in the different schools of thought which have used them: on the one hand conservative, Christian, right-wing Prussians agreed that history had indeed culminated in a world in which they had power (until the 1860s). On the other hand, the rising historical materialists of the Marxist school took from the same theories a doctrine of revolution, atheism, and dynamic change.

History did not stay in the university, however. As Popkin notes, the discipline's 'prestige influenced politics and culture more than ever before — or probably would do again.' It was accepted and approved that historians would also be politicians or their advisers, and conversely that politicians should be educated in their own nation's past and that of their neighbours. This acceptance was, in part, no more than the normal expectation that those who represent us should share our interests, and history was a popular as well as an educated interest. It led to a series of enormous, multi-volume national 'epic history' in which the protagonist was not the spirit of the times or a man of genius, but the common folk of the nation. Sentimental, glorious, highly colourful and shaped as a series of loosely-joined episodes, works like Augustine Thierry's *Norman Conquest of England* and Jules Michelet's *History of France* and *History of the French Revolution* were hardly critical history, but they were enormously popular.

Thomas Macauley was both an MP and author of a hugely popular history of England, which promoted the idea that England's rise to imperial power was the definition of progress, and the means by which this progress would be spread to the corners of the Earth.

In Britain, the Great Reform Act of 1832 made people particularly interested in the Glorious Revolution of 1688 and the French Revolution of 1789, an interest to which Thomas Carlyle catered in his magisterial *The French Revolution: A History*. The writer and Whig MP Thomas Macauley chased this up with *The History of England*, which established what we now refer to as the Whig interpretation of history, emphasising constitutional democracy, moderate secularism, and technological innovation as the benchmarks of human progress.

Historical fiction as the progenitor of 'Historism'

Almost certainly, Historism owed at least some of its origin, certainly its acceptance, to Romanticism in literature and art at the beginning of the 19th century. Changing fashions in art favoured the style that we now call 'medievalist' – the romantic, photo-realistic depiction of how the nineteenth century imagined the Middle Ages. Queen Victoria and the Prince Consort were particularly fond of this style, and many of the buildings which bear their names are 'neo-Gothic' or medievalist: the many works of Augustus Pugin and George Gilbert Scott continue to surround churchgoers and university students with Romanesque and neo-Gothic influences.

Above all others, interest in the past was exploited by the Scottish historical novelist Walter Scott (1771-1832). Scott not only popularized the past (particularly that period known as the High Middle Ages) but wrote so convincingly about it that historians felt compelled to assert the difference between his fictions and their narratives. Scott defended himself in the preface to his famous novel *Ivanhoe* (about a Saxon warrior who fights against the Norman French Brian de Bois-Gilbert for the hand of the beautiful and impeccably Anglo-Saxon Rowena – while Brian loves the exotic, Jewish, Rebecca). He refuted the charge that by 'intermingling fiction with truth, I am polluting the well of history with modern inventions and impressing upon the rising generation false ideas of the age which I describe.'

Edwin Landseer's portrait of Queen Victoria and Prince Albert in 'medieval' dress for the Bal Costumé of 12 May 1842.

Scott insisted that his study of historical records – many of which he purchased, making a valuable private collection which scholars still consult today – underpinned his narratives. He wrote that he sought to understand

> the private lives of our ancestors, to write about the past in ways that the modern reader will not find himself... much trammelled by the repulsive dryness of mere antiquity.

Nineteenth-century arguments about the historical validity of novels foreshadowed modern historians' objections that novelists and filmmakers distort the past to make their commercially-oriented products 'accessible'. And as Scott did, present-day novelists and filmmakers contend that their works enliven the past for otherwise disinterested audiences. The past, particularly the medieval past, was woven into the nineteenth century in a more thorough-going way, however, which is evident in the art, architecture, and craft of the period. The Pre-Raphaelite school of writers and artists, the Gothic Revival architectural movement, and the Arts and Crafts group headed by William Morris are all evidence of a popular and commercially-successful preference for an 'updated past' in western Europe, and even the United States.

Schloss Neuschwanstein was built in the 1880s in a manner evoking a lost Teutonic medieval period. Walt Disney appropriated it for the Disney emblem, and this watercolour was painted by Adolf Hitler in 1914.

Think laterally

2. Identify some benefits and drawbacks to historians of studying historical fiction.

_____

_____

_____

_____

Historism

The insistence that each nation and culture should be understood on its own terms was fundamentally different from the lofty, de-contextualized philosophical history of previous centuries. In addition, increasingly rigorous treatment of sources – which were being published in edited collections by scholarly and antiquarian societies for the first time – meant that the practice of history-writing became increasingly professional and elite. Human life was now accepted to be intrinsically historical, and the value of the discipline was recognized by the academy.

In time, the nineteenth century came to label such an approach as 'Historism', which the German historian Friedrich Meinecke defined in 1936 as

> the substitution of a process of individualising observation for a generalising view of human forces in history...The world and all its life take on a new aspect once one has become accustomed to looking at them along these new lines.

Historism was attractive because it acknowledged two things which we now take as simply common sense: everyone's experience is slightly different, and that everything that is, is *as* it is because of what it was. In other words, human society is innately historical. To write about this fairly and accurately, however, required new tools and a rigorous, consistent method of using them. The first to produce this method was the Danish-German scholar Barthold Neibuhr (*left* 1776-1831), upon whose work the 'father of them all' Leopold von Ranke built the discipline that we call History.

Neibuhr devised a two-fold method of source-handling which we call *philological criticism*. This involved *textual* or *external criticism*: analysing sources into their component parts, then placing those parts in a chronological sequence which allowed the historian to trace the transmission and composition of the document and the account it contained. Only a thorough knowledge of all the sources *and* the components from which they were built – many of which could only be inferred since they no longer existed – allowed a critic to do this, and the increasing number of learned societies and antiquarians who were collecting, translating, and transcribing sources made this more possible. The second element of Neibuhr's source-handling method was the *internal criticism* of the text, in which the author's context, perspective, and language affected his account.

Although many 'historists' were both nationalists and conservatives, the importance of the past to the current state of things was of vital importance to Marxism. One of the best descriptions of a practical historist approach was given by Vladimir Lenin, who said that its basic principle is:

> not to forget the underlying historical connection, to examine every question from the standpoint of how the given phenomenon arose in history and what principal stages this phenomenon passed through in its

development, and, from the standpoint of its development, to examine what the given thing has become today.

Meinecke used the metaphor of germ-plasm (a theory of heredity developed during the nineteenth century by August Weismann) to describe macroscopic ideas about society:

Individual historical development is no mere evolution of tendencies already present in the germ-cell. Rather does it possess a large measure of plasticity, of capacity to change and be regenerated as it is worked upon by the ever-changing forces of time. That is why the individual and the general are so inextricably interwoven, and why the current of historical development is a unity. Otherwise we should have a countless number of different evolutionary processes.

Colossus: Leopold von Ranke

Modern historians restrict Walter Scott to 'historical fiction', but perhaps the greatest historiographer of the nineteenth century, the German Leopold von Ranke (*left,* 1795-1886), attributed his desire to pursue history to Scott's novels and the Romantic poetry and philosophy of Gottfriend von Herder. Ranke taught at the recently-founded University of Berlin for some sixty years, a longevity which enabled him to teach and influence several generations of historians, both German and foreign. Despite his attraction to novels about individuals from different ranks in society, Ranke was only firmly interested in the *staatengeschichte,* or political history, through which he aimed over his long career to trace 'the conception and composition of a history of mankind'.

He acknowledged Thucydides, Niebuhr, and Fichte as his own influences, but what prompted him to write history was a comparison of the two principal historians of sixteenth-century Italy: Francesco Guicciardini and Paolo Giovio. Ranke found that the two accounts were so completely different that he determined to write his own, to resolve the problem. *Histories of the Latin and Teutonic Peoples 1494-1514* was published when Ranke was only 29 years old and it is important to note that this work, and the career which ensued, had come about because of engagement with other, previous historians. In Ranke's academic origins, and his own influences, John Tosh's idea that 'history is an argument without end', an engagement with other accounts and perspectives, is apparent. No historian works in a vacuum.

Through his books *On the Tasks of the Historian* (1821) and *Theory and Practice of History* (1835) Ranke is remembered, above all else, for an aphorism defining history - *wie es eigentlich gewesen,* or 'how it really was', without anger, favouritism, or bombast. In this aphorism, Ranke suggested that it is the historian's task to represent and thus judge the past according to the principles of *that* time rather than by the standards of their own time, including the idea of 'universal laws' which are, in fact, formulated by one period. Underpinning Ranke's view of history was the belief that every era was *unmittelbar zu Gott*, that is *immediate to God*.

Accordingly, von Ranke emphasised the historian's obligation to use contemporary documentary sources as much as possible to inform their knowledge of events. This was made easier because printing and archives had made these considerably more accessible to scholars. Yet possession of primary evidence could lead historians to a false sense of security. Even physical possession of the sole example of an original document was not the same as transparent access to the past. Most sources are edited, translated, anthologized, and otherwise handled such that what we use is not *the past in and of itself* but a map or landscape of it, as Bartold Niebuhr had commented.

Think laterally

3. Briefly give an example of an act which was received with horror in its own time, and approbation in ours.

___
___
___
___

Clarify

4. For your own understanding, briefly explain Niebuhr's distinction.

___
___
___

It seemed to Ranke that the entire history of the past cried out to be rewritten, a decision which resulted in the creation of the university research *Seminar* and historical journal (the *Historische Zeitschrift,* first published in 1859 and still a first-rank vehicle for peer-reviewed historical research). Ranke understood that historians tended to become absorbed in the details of a single past event because of the 'pleasure in the particular for itself'. While he emphasised that 'the strict presentation of the facts, contingent and unattractive though they may be, is undoubtedly the supreme law', he also conceded that a dry chronicle of isolated facts was both unsatisfactory and unpalatable. Therefore, the historian had to present the facts to show the 'unity and progress of events.' to seek the broader meaning – the significance, in other words, of the particular to the bigger narrative. He also emphasised the historian's duty to keep accessible records of where their claims originated – that is, in the sources, which were now footnoted to provide a kind of metatext or double-chronicle, and what evaluation these sources had accrued. While not entirely original in this (after all, both featured in Herodotus' *Histories* and Gibbon's *Memoirs*) Ranke produced a *mis-en-page* which has become synonymous with a scholarly, academic style.

Clarify

5. List Ranke's requirements for history-writing.

_____
_____
_____
_____
_____

Ranke's work provoked a range of responses from historians and historiographers. His Swiss student Jacob Burckhardt criticized the political emphasis of Ranke's history. In the next generation, the British historian G.P. Gooch, in *History and Historians in the 19th-Century* (1913) judged Ranke 'the master of us all.' In the 1980s Ernst Breisach reckoned von Ranke as the 'key figure' in defining a modern approach because of his contributions to historical methodology and 'the universality of his historical vision.' More recent historiographers such as Peter Reilly, Donald Kelly and Anthony Grafton have questioned Ranke's originality, suggesting that his historism and critical methodology simply systematized trends and methods emerging in historical writing since the Renaissance.

If Ranke contributed anything to the revolution in History it was formalising the academic activities, research seminars, archives, journals and associations of historians. He asserted their fundamental difference, both in ethos and praxis, from literature and philosophy. The University of Cambridge established a fully autonomous Historical Tripos from 1875, and the American Historical Association founded in 1884 and *English Historical Review* (1886) are examples of the systematic association and production of history and historians. Charles-Victor Langlois and Charles Seignobos' *Introduction to the Study of History* (1897) was the 'how-to' manual of Rankean scholarship and remains a (much-copied) manual for tertiary history-students. Its chapter headings characterize the intellectual operations we use when we 'do' history, as well as the places we find the raw materials:

I. *The Search for Documents*
II. *Auxiliary Sciences*
III. *Analytical Operations*
IV. *Textual Criticism*
V. *Critical Investigation of Authorship*
VI. *Critical Classification Of Sources*
VII. *Critical Scholarship And Scholars*
VIII. *Interpretative Criticism (Hermeneutic)*
IX. *The Negative Internal Criticism Of The Good Faith And Accuracy Of Authors*
X. *The Determination Of Particular Facts*
XI. *General Conditions Of Historical Construction*
XII. *The Grouping Of Facts*
XIII. *Constructive Reasoning*
XIV. *The Construction Of General Formulæ*
XV. *Exposition*

However Ranke is assessed, by the last decades of the nineteenth century history had pervaded European and Western culture to an unprecedented extent. While few contemporaries read scholarly articles in the Rankean tradition – after all university-trained historians were still few and far between – by the end of the nineteenth century general readers could assume that works of history rested on a solid basis of consistent and accessible scholarship.

Responses and Reactions to Rankean Historicism

Ranke's methods and structures came to represent not only a particular type of academic respectability, but a political conservatism, at least in Germany. Nonetheless, in a very Rankean irony, Ranke's own thesis about the nature of history inevitably spawned its own antithesis. Stemming in part from the reaction of Friedrich Nietzsche, and in part from a revival of the ideas of Giambattista Vico by Wilhelm Dilthey and Benedetto Croce, idealist history developed as an alternative to the dry, documentary tradition of Ranke.

Clarify

6. Ranke v Nietzsche is one important thesis/antithesis pairing by which the conversation about history and historical method is moved along. Write down other antithetical pairings which you've encountered so far.

_____

_____

_____

_____

_____

Karl Marx and Friedrich Engels

Karl Marx's contribution to Western thought was greater than simply opposing Ranke, and indeed many people who have never heard of Ranke know the name of Marx. Nonetheless, Marx represents the positivistic school of thought which rejected Ranke's 'heaping up facts' view of history, and so can usefully be thought of as one of the many who responded to Rankean historicism.

Marx and his collaborator Friedrich Engels took the tools of Hegelian dialectic and applied them to a materialistic view of history. There was no point, they said, in claiming that history was about the ideas people have had and how they changed. None of that could really be grasped – it couldn't be *positively* proved. The basic tenor of human social life was material and economic. First of all we have access to things, we make them, we struggle for more of them, and we suffer from the lack of them. In their book *The*

Holy Family, Marx and Engels had claimed that 'history is nothing but the activity of man pursing his goals.' Only once we are satisfied for a while in the level of material wealth that we possess can we have ideas. However, the human drive to acquire more, and particularly more profit, means that we are never satisfied, and so history is really the story of people's struggle to acquire more things and the means of producing them. Because individuals are relatively powerless, this struggle is waged between groups defined by their control of the means to produce things – these groups are social classes. Like Vico, Marx saw human society as a process going through different stages – but for Marx the stages were determined by the relationship of classes. There was a slave-owning economy, a feudal stage, and a bourgeois period and each hegemony created an ideology which sought to perpetuate it. Eventually members of the subordinated group saw through this ideology and attempted to overthrow the powerful class – which was powerful because it had appropriated the surplus value created by the labour of the people.

It was a powerfully convincing narrative, one of epic scope and deceptive simplicity – and one which was greeted with some skepticism by the Rankeans who pointed out that specific historical situations were usually much more complex than this. Marxist dialectical materialism was an interesting and persuasive way to analyse current social situations and to jockey for change in the future, but it has also been accused of pre-determining the narrative of the past to suit itself. Marx's contribution to historiography was to bring the forces of economic activity and the social activity which facilitates and explains it into the foreground of history, instead of the Rankean focus on the state and its machinery. Marxist historical narrative paved the way for the twentieth century's interest in history of the masses, and history 'from below.'

Friedrich Nietzche

Friedrich Nietzsche's essay 'The Use and Abuse of History' (1873) treated Ranke's claims to objectivity with scepticism. He argued that this heavily academic, rather dry historical approach risked causing intellectual life to atrophy and degenerate. Further, it was not as objective as it claimed because we tend to construct the sort of past that we would prefer to have had, rather than the one we actually did have. This was all part of Nietzsche's wider argument about the morally and ethically superior person, who can look unpleasant realities in the face and overcome them rather than lying to themselves about the facts, or 'writing around' problems. As the historian E.H. Carr would later point out, the psychology of the historian contributes to the way they view the past, and how they reproduce it in writing.

It is important to remember that Nietzsche was a classical philologist who had moved into philosophy, and who wrote in a highly ambiguous, epigrammatic style which is regularly appropriated by many different kinds of argument. Although Nietzsche had been trained in classical philology, his work offers a *response* (usually a rejection) to historical concepts. While he dilated on the idea of the transmission of morals through time, he was not primarily a historian.

In his essay Nietzsche identified three types of history, which had different purposes and could produce different problems. The Monumental was history-writing in the heroic tradition; celebrating 'greatness' and 'big things' – important men and events, which it recounted in an epic style. The Antiquarian dilated on the past for its own sake and as Jeremy Popkin says, 'provided an identity but was hostile to change and development'. There was also the Critical, which 'brings the past to a tribunal, interrogates it and condemns it.' Anthony Jensen sums up Nietzsche's approach to this taxonomy by saying:

> Each type of historian and their accordant way of representing the past has its advantages and disadvantages for themselves and for the cultures in which they live, but none is able to represent the past as it 'really' was since into each of their judgments intrudes their psychologically-determined desires and interests.

Wilhelm Dilthey

The philosopher Wilhelm Dilthey (*left* 1833-1911), took his cue from Giambattista Vico's distinction between 'human' and 'natural' sciences. Dilthey argued that the human element of history meant that it was not material which could be approached 'objectively'. Instead, he said, historians drew on their own experience as people in the world to understand other people who lived in the world in the past. Dilthey's first course of study was theology, which may explain his emphasis on the individual's lived experience and the relationship between the visible and invisible parts of an event.

Rather than Ranke's objective-scientific view of historical material, Dilthey believed that the similarity in nature between the historian and his subject meant that the discipline was an imaginative and subjective one. We imagine and re-enact the past; it lives in our mind's eye, not in documentary evidence, which merely provides the raw material for this imaginative engagement. In his 1894 essay 'Ideas for a Descriptive and Analytic Psychology' Dilthey said that

> We explain through purely intellectual processes, but we understand through the cooperation of all the powers of the mind activated by apprehension.

When we speak to older people, our criticism of their actions is often met with the response, 'You don't know; you weren't there.' This is effectively what Dilthey is saying about Ranke's approach to history: we cannot presume to know what it was really like simply by studying an account or looking at sources.

Wilhelm Windelband and Max Weber

In the meantime, Wilhelm Windelband (1848-1915) attempted to steer a middle course between Ranke's insistence on history as a science which dealt with objective and external material and Croce's conception of history as an act of imaginative reconstruction which engages subjectively with internal objects of knowledge. To do this he had to show that the so-called 'cultural sciences' like history, sociology and the arts were not intellectually subsidiary to logic, maths, and natural sciences.

Windelband invented the terms nomothetic (for disciplines which are generalizing and law-positing like chemistry and physics), and idiographic (disciplines which dealt with unique, un-reproducible events like geology and astronomy). Because the human mind is not purely law-positing or generalizing, and deals all the time with constantly-changing environments which demand an ability to deal with the unique, we need both types of knowledge and thought – the idiographic, which informs and the nomothetic, which demonstrates. Windelband's view was thus a synthesis of the Rankean understanding of history as science which dealt with the objective and had certain methodological laws, and the idealist vision which saw it as unique and partially determined by the subjectivity of individuals.

Max Weber (*left* 1864-1920) was an important proponent of the social-scientific approach to the past – so much so that he is remembered as a sociologist rather than a historian. He argued that understanding actions in the past was impossible without an understanding of the value-system which informed those actions. Empirical means could not explain why an action was taken or what its significance was to the actors – they could only measure its tangible effects. To do this, historians had to engage imaginatively and critically with the culture and values of the society they study. (This is not the same as saying that history only exists in the imagination of the historian.)

Weber's most famous book, *The Protestant Ethic and the Spirit of Capitalism* (1905), shows this approach. Although the growth of capitalism in northern Europe can be demonstrated empirically, Weber's question – what, in the human actors who fuelled capitalist economic trends, caused it to grow – was about immeasurable ideas behind the data. He concluded that the values we associate with Protestantism such as hard work, frugality, financial rationalism, cultural asceticism, and literacy, lay behind market-driven capitalism.

J.B. Bury and G.M. Trevelyan

The debate about Rankean approaches to history was not only an academic subject. Because the skills and attitudes fostered by the German 'scientific' school were only available to those who had undergone an extremely academic education, the Rankean tradition had implications for the sort of people who could do history at all.

In his inaugural lecture as regius professor at Cambridge in 1902 the Irish-born classicist J.B. Bury *(left)*, who was possessed of exactly the kind of highly erudite background which Ranke's approach rewarded, exhorted the students and fellows to continue 'heaping up material and arranging it according to the best methods we know,' and was adamant that history should not be treated as a literary fiction in the style of Sir Walter Scott, however great the research behind novels might be. Bury contributed two important ideas which stood as a corrective to some of the increasing specialization of the discipline: one was that no period is more important than another, and the second was that the Rankean *staatengeschichte* must yield to a more comprehensive study of the story of man in society. Bury also argued that we must implement a thoroughly 'historical' character in national education. He noted that our conception of the past was one of the most important factors in our practical development of plans and visions for the future.

Few, by Bury's time, would have argued with these ideas. The sticking point was the rejection of history's imaginative and literary character, the idea of story as a fundamentally artistic undertaking. History, Bury said, was a science:

> I may remind you that history is not a branch of literature. The facts of history, like the facts of geology or astronomy, can supply material for literary art; for manifest reasons they lend themselves to artistic representation far more readily than those of the natural sciences; but to clothe the story of human society in a literary dress is no more the part of a historian as a historian, than it is the part of an astronomer as an astronomer to present in an artistic shape the story of the stars ... [history] is a science, no less and no more.

A direct response to Bury came in the form of George Macaulay Trevelyan's *Clio: A Muse* (1903). Trevelyan (*left*), who was Regius Professor of History at Cambridge more than twenty years after Bury, warned that historians in the Rankean tradition were making themselves and the discipline inaccessible to a wider readership. Trevelyan further cautioned that:

> Until quite recent times, historical writing was not merely the mutual conversation of scholars with one another but was the means of spreading far and wide throughout all reading classes a love and knowledge of history, an elevated and critical patriotism and certain qualities of mind and heart.

Yet Trevelyan believed that history's capacity to reach people lay in its ability to tell a great story about great human achievements. In 'the most important part of its business, history is not a scientific deduction, but an imaginative guess at the most likely generalisations.' Ironically, both Bury and Trevelyan were ardent followers of John Dalberg-Acton, Lord Acton, also a follower of Ranke, and also a professor at Cambridge. E.H. Carr wrote that Trevelyan was one of the last historians of the Whig tradition, with its focus on progress, the optimistic story of human growth, and the use of history as a narrative placed in the public service. Trevelyan recognized that narration was the key to history's appeal and utility, and that historians, far from being remote and disinterested 'scientists' had to have brilliant imaginative powers, humour, insight and sympathy – anything else was to have 'more knowledge of facts...less understanding of man.'

Emile Durkheim and Henri Bar

Similar reactions occurred in France, between Emile Durkheim (*left*) and Henri Barr (1863-1914), who insisted on the importance of sociological factors to the study of history – so much so that, like Weber, both men are remembered primarily as sociologists rather than historians. Their belief in the importance of interdisciplinary studies would lead to the foundation of the *Annales* school in France before the Second World War. One of their associates, another sociologist, François Simiand, listed what he perceived as three fatal flaws in the way that historians looked at their material. One was a fixation with political history to the detriment of other elements of the social past. The second was a greater interest in individuals rather than facts and events. The third was the habit of tracing how institutions developed through time rather than focusing on their significance to the society which contextualized them. The *Annales* school, and its journal, would seek to address these three problems.

Charles Peirce and William James

In the USA a type of philosophy known as Pragmatism was promulgated by Charles Peirce (*left*) and William James, which responded in part to the Rankean belief that history needed to be rewritten using a scholarly method so deterministic that no rewriting would ever be needed again. Against Ranke's apparent belief in some absolute truth which historians could get at simply by precision of method, the Pragmatists focused on the utility and practical limits of history, contending that at some point we reach an understanding of a situation or event which is as fair and accurate as it's likely to get – and at that point we should stop and consider the matter closed. Peirce's pragmatist perspective was acutely conscious that the spread of literacy during the 19th century had greatly enlarged the reading audience with whom the popular history genre enjoyed great success. James Harvey Robinson suggested that there was a 'New History', a scholarship which dealt with all aspects of society in order to prepare its audience for 'intelligent social activity.'

Think laterally

7. Choose ONE responder to Ranke from the men listed. Explain their view of history *in your own words*. Then explain:

a) with what aspect of Ranke's beliefs they disagreed

b) which one you think is right, and

c) why.

Make sure you write your answers in a way that lets you share them in class.

CONCEPT FOCUS 5: NATIONALIST HISTORY

Nationalist history can be characterized by:
- a focus on the nation, rather than dynasties, individuals or ethnic groups
- a sense of the epic past of the nation leading to a 'manifest destiny' through progress;
- highly-coloured vignettes
- highly partisan treatment of the subject
- a confident and even bombastic tone and other rhetorical techniques
- dramatic and frequently supersized characters, who are presented with exaggerated virtues and vices
- description rather than explanation

Read the extract below, from Macaulay's *History of Enland from the Accession of James II* (1848). It describes the treatment of Charles I, which led to the period of the Commonwealth. Identify the features of nationalist history in Macaulay's text.

> When a country is in the situation in which England then was, when the kingly office is regarded with love and veneration, but the person who fills that office is hated and distrusted, it should seem that the course which ought to be taken is obvious. The dignity of the office should be preserved: the person should be discarded. Thus our ancestors acted in 1399 and in 1689. Had there been, in 1642, any man occupying a position similar to that which Henry of Lancaster occupied at the time of the deposition of Richard the Second, and which William of Orange occupied at the time of the deposition of James the Second, it is probable that the Houses would have changed the dynasty, and would have made no formal change in the constitution. The new King, called to the throne by their choice, and dependent on their support, would have been under the necessity of governing in conformity with their wishes and opinions. But there was no prince of the blood royal in the parliamentary party; and, though that party contained many men of high rank and many men of eminent ability, there was none who towered so conspicuously above the rest that he could be proposed as a candidate for the crown. As there was to be a King, and as no new King could be found, it was necessary to leave the regal title to Charles. Only one course, therefore, was left: and that was to disjoin the regal title from the regal prerogatives.
>
> The change which the Houses proposed to make in our institutions, though it seems exorbitant, when distinctly set forth and digested into articles of capitulation, really amounts to little more than the change which, in the next generation, was effected by the Revolution. It is true that, at the Revolution, the sovereign was not deprived by law of the power of naming his ministers: but it is equally true that, since the Revolution, no minister has been able to retain office six months in opposition to the sense of the House of Commons. It is true that the sovereign still possesses the power of creating peers, and the more important power of the sword: but it is equally true that in the exercise of these powers the sovereign has, ever since the Revolution, been guided by advisers who possess the confidence of the representatives of the nation. In fact, the leaders of the Roundhead party in 1642, and the statesmen who, about half a century later, effected the Revolution, had exactly the same object in view. That object was to terminate the contest between the Crown and the Parliament, by giving to the Parliament a supreme control over the executive administration. The statesmen of the Revolution effected this indirectly by changing the dynasty. The Roundheads of 1642, being unable to change the dynasty, were compelled to take a direct course towards their end.

We cannot, however, wonder that the demands of the opposition, importing as they did a complete and formal transfer to the Parliament of powers which had always belonged to the Crown, should have shocked that great party of which the characteristics are respect for constitutional authority and dread of violent innovation. That party had recently been in hopes of obtaining by peaceable means the ascendency in the House of Commons; but every such hope had been blighted. The duplicity of Charles had made his old enemies irreconcileable, had driven back into the ranks of the disaffected a crowd of moderate men who were in the very act of coming over to his side, and had so cruelly mortified his best friends that they had for a time stood aloof in silent shame and resentment. Now, however, the constitutional Royalists were forced to make their choice between two dangers; and they thought it their duty rather to rally round a prince whose past conduct they condemned, and whose word inspired them with little confidence, than to suffer the regal office to be degraded, and the polity of the realm to be entirely remodelled. With such feelings, many men whose virtues and abilities would have done honour to any cause, ranged themselves on the side of the King.

In August 1642 the sword was at length drawn; and soon, in almost every shire of the kingdom, two hostile factions appeared in arms against each other. It is not easy to say which of the contending parties was at first the more formidable. The Houses commanded London and the counties round London, the fleet, the navigation of the Thames, and most of the large towns and seaports. They had at their disposal almost all the military stores of the kingdom, and were able to raise duties, both on goods imported from foreign countries, and on some important products of domestic industry. The King was ill provided with artillery and ammunition. The taxes which he laid on the rural districts occupied by his troops produced, it is probable, a sum far less than that which the Parliament drew from the city of London alone. He relied, indeed, chiefly, for pecuniary aid, on the munificence of his opulent adherents. Many of these mortgaged their land, pawned their jewels, and broke up their silver chargers and christening bowls, in order to assist him. But experience has fully proved that the voluntary liberality of individuals, even in times of the greatest excitement, is a poor financial resource when compared with severe and methodical taxation, which presses on the willing and unwilling alike.

Charles, however, had one advantage, which, if he had used it well, would have more than compensated for the want of stores and money, and which, notwithstanding his mismanagement, gave him, during some months, a superiority in the war. His troops at first fought much better than those of the Parliament. Both armies, it is true, were almost entirely composed of men who had never seen a field of battle. Nevertheless, the difference was great. The Parliamentary ranks were filled with hirelings whom want and idleness had induced to enlist. Hampden's regiment was regarded as one of the best; and even Hampden's regiment was described by Cromwell as a mere rabble of tapsters and serving men out of place. The royal army, on the other hand, consisted in great part of gentlemen, high spirited, ardent, accustomed to consider dishonour as more terrible than death, accustomed to fencing, to the use of fire arms, to bold riding, and to manly and perilous sport, which has been well called the image of war. Such gentlemen, mounted on their favourite horses, and commanding little bands composed of their younger brothers, grooms, gamekeepers, and huntsmen, were, from the very first day on which they took the field, qualified to play their part with credit in a skirmish. The steadiness, the prompt obedience, the mechanical precision of movement, which are characteristic of the regular soldier, these gallant volunteers never attained. But they were at first opposed to enemies as undisciplined as themselves, and far less active, athletic, and daring. For a time, therefore, the Cavaliers were successful in almost every encounter.

8. Write a brief reflection on this statement: 'The past changes each time we look at it; it changes because we have looked at it.'

Reading task 5

Reading tasks from now on will require you to begin basic historical research by locating the rest of the text in a print or digital library. You should look carefully at the website and note the institution from which it comes, what historical project it is attached to, and why that particular university or publication might provide access to this text. This is an important way to recognize ideological affiliations in universities and working groups of historians which shape historiographical discourse.

Read this extract from Ranke's preface to his *History of the Latin and Teutonic Nations*, written when he was only twenty-nine years old.

The purpose of an historian depends upon his point of view. About my viewpoint in this volume, two things must be said. First, I regard the Latin and Germanic peoples as a unit. This notion differs from three analogous concepts: the concept of a universal Christendom (which would include even the Armenians); the concept of Europe (for the Turks there are Asiatics, and the Russian empire embraces the whole of northern Asia and cannot be understood without investigating and penetrating a complete range of Asiatic affairs); and, the most analogous concept, the concept of Latin Christianity (for Slavic, Lithuanian, and Magyar races belonging to the latter have their own special and peculiar nature which I shall not include here).

By touching upon what is foreign to this unity only where necessary and only as a passing and subordinate matter, the author will remain close to the racially kindred nations of either purely Germanic or Latin-Germanic origin whose history forms the heart of all modern history.

Now read the rest of the extract at the German History in Documents and Images site, an initiative of the German Historical Institute in Washington, DC.

http://ghdi.ghi-dc.org/sub_document.cfm?document_id=358

9. Identify, by highlighting or underlining, the key historiographical concepts discussed so far.

10. Which historical concept is most important to Ranke's understanding of his subject, the Latin and Teutonic nations?

___
___
___
___
___
___
___
___
___
___

11. Which historiographical concept is most important to the way he believes history should be written?

12. Write a personal reaction to Ranke's statement in this extract – with which bits of his philosophy do you agree and with which do you disagree?

13. Why might the German Historical Institute, based in Washington, have made this text digitally available in English now?

Notes

Chapter revision statement

Write a list of the key points from this chapter.

_____
_____
_____
_____
_____
_____
_____
_____
_____
_____

Use the list to write a short statement about important features in the discipline of history during the period studied in this chapter.

_____
_____
_____
_____
_____
_____
_____

Notes

_____
_____
_____
_____
_____
_____
_____
_____

Chapter 6: The beginning of disillusionment

Pre-empting the postmodernists of the late twentieth century, Charles Beard wrote that 'Whatever active purification the historian may perform, he yet remains human, a creature of time, place, circumstance, interests, predilections, culture.' The fact that every historian is always working within some particular time and culture meant that complete objectivity was impossible. The First and Second World wars caused an enormous loss of faith in many areas of life, including academic life. History was no exception; there is a sense of withdrawal into the academy and a reinforcing of history as a specialist discipline which was no longer prepared to make great statements about human nature, national character, and the possibility of finding some objective truth.

Unless they actually served at the front like the French historian Marc Bloch, academic historians treated the First World War as simply another European war no different in kind or even scale than the conflicts of the nineteenth century. As Jeremy Popkin points out,

> as late as October 1918 when the German army was telling its government that it was on the point of military defeat, Friedrich Meinecke, apparently ignorant of impending social, economic, and political collapse, continued to hold the view that Germany could obtain favourable peace terms including territorial gains.

Others took a more dramatic attitude, taking descriptive phrases like 'the war to end all wars' to their natural conclusion and suggesting that the scale of devastation over (what in retrospect seemed) relatively unimportant causes meant the end of Western civilisation. Oswald Spengler's *Decline of the West* (1918-1922) was influential in both Germany and the victorious countries because its focus on the defeat chimed with the mood in Britain of pyrrhic victory. Drawing on the narrative of decline, Spengler (*left*) argued that Western civilization had reached its zenith around 1800. This was when it had 'realized the complete sum of its possibilities in the shape of peoples, languages, creeds, arts, states, and sciences, and thereupon goes back into the primitive psyche from which it originally emerged.' After this, the spontaneity of a culture at its height gives way to 'mere' civilization which kills itself.

Spengler's suspicion towards the propagandistic media represented a sense that the integrity and well-being of the individual could no longer compete with the machinations of larger commercial and ideological concerns:

> To-day we live so cowed under the bombardment of this intellectual artillery [the media] that hardly anyone can attain to the inward detachment that is required for a clear view of the monstrous drama. The will-to-power operating under a pure democratic disguise has finished off its masterpiece so well that the object's sense of freedom is actually flattered by the most thorough-going enslavement that has ever existed.

 A more optimistic attempt to set out the pattern which underpinned human history was the British historian Arnold Toynbee's massive *A Study of History* (1934-1961). Toynbee used several binaries to express his perception of history's moving forces. Human beings lived in either 'societies' which were primitive, or Civilizations – their difference from societies was the only thing that civilizations had in common. Civilizations arose from the combination of a creative minority or elite, and 'goldilocks' environment – one which was neither indolence-inducing nor too harsh. Civilizations survive and grow by successfully navigating Challenge and Response mechanisms. They are also guided by Withdrawal and Return cycles, where some people or groups withdraw in order to gain clarity, and then return to enlighten and lead the rest of the group. Finally, when they do disintegrate, civilizations experience Schism in Body Social and Soul.

Toynbee answered the charge that his view was too deterministic by saying that 'We are not doomed to make history repeat itself; it is open to us, through our own efforts, to give history, in our case, some new and unprecedented turn.' This was different in tone to Spengler's belief that there was only a series of rises and falls. Toynbee was one of the most-read historians of his time, but his twelve-volume work (the first six volumes were abridged into a single volume for a mass market) faded from academic approval extremely quickly because of his preference for myths and allegories over hard data.

In one respect, however, Toynbee and Spengler were both seminal: they both recognized mass media's power to communicate and shape values within society. There has been a long hiatus since an academic historian has attempted to write history of Toynbee's vast scope, but the recent vogue for 'Big History' such as David Christian's *Maps of Time* (2004) is reminiscent of both Spengler and Toynbee, though entirely different in the type of material used and the vision of human society.

While these historians worked within a single overarching pattern, others concentrated on more limited questions, for example, the controversy resulting from the war-guilt clause in the Versailles Treaty of 1919. As Popkin notes, newly-available documents about European international relations 'stimulated a seemingly-endless revisionist controversy which shook confidence that history's developing research methods could ever determine a final truth about the past.' One explanation for this perpetual deferral of a 'final truth' was the recognition that different historians ask different questions, make different connections, and have different agenda towards the material.

As a proponent of America's so-called progressive school, Beard's 'proto-relativist' position (which was Peirce and Barr's Pragmatist philosophy applied to History) was shared by Carl Becker. His 1931 presidential address to the American Historical Association was titled 'Everyman His Own Historian', suggesting that history necessarily adapts to meet the needs of an ever-changing present. In his own study of philosophical history, Becker wrote that

> All historical writing, even the most honest, is unconsciously subjective, since every age is bound, in spite of itself, to make the dead perform whatever tricks it finds necessary for its own peace of mind ... Since

history is not an objective reality, but only an imaginative reconstruction of vanished events, the pattern that appears useful and agreeable to one generation is never entirely so to the next.

The Positivist belief in total objectivity was impossible; the Rankean attempt to tell the story of the State without rancour was no longer likely or even worthy, given the outcome of WWI. Even the fixity of historical narratives was no longer taken for granted.

Think laterally

1. Assuming it was even possible, in what ways might complete objectivity be undesirable in the discipline of history?

_____

_____

_____

_____

More revolutionary history

The perception that it was appropriate to rewrite history for each generation was elevated to a principle in the emerging Soviet Union. Their government called on historians to follow Karl Marx and rewrite history in order to combat 'bourgeois' critics. The most influential example of this was Leon Trotsky's *Russian Revolution* (1932), in which Trotsky (*left*) and his colleague Lenin both played significant roles. The Marxist philosophy which underpinned Trotsky's historical vision presented interesting historiographical challenges, particularly understanding the role of change in history. Marxism's view of change as a perpetual process caused by the continual struggle for greater access to material wealth meant that instead of seeing change as an *outcome* of historical events, change and history were largely synonymous. Trotsky wrote that:

> We seek to uncover behind the events changes in the collective consciousness. We reject wholesale references to the "spontaneity" of the movement, references which in most cases explain nothing and teach nobody. Revolutions take place according to certain laws. This does not mean that the masses in action are aware of the laws of revolution, but it does mean that the changes in mass consciousness are not accidental, but are subject to an objective necessity which is capable of theoretic explanation, and thus makes both prophecy and leadership possible.

Similar developments in rewriting history also occurred in Germany after 1933 as National Socialist historians revised and re-narrated history in ways that supported the Nazi message.

Benedetto Croce

Benedetto Croce (*left* 1866-1952) was a stringent opponent of the Italian Fascists, and his visions of history and its place in the development of the whole person reflect a more positive tone than Spengler or other post-WWI writers. Croce develops Dilthey's thesis about the importance of imagination, suggesting that the past really only exists in the mind of those who study it because they are re-enacting it through imagination as they engage with sources. This means that the past only ever exists in the present, because we're creating it as we go.

A member of the Italian government in the early 1920s Croce was a vocal critic of Mussolini's fascist party, which co-opted and recontextualized the ideas, emblems, and structures from previous eras, particularly ancient Rome, to articulate a nationalistic and authoritarian political attitude (which the Roman empire had rarely, if ever, used). In this way, fascism of the 1930s sought to legitimize itself by drawing on historical sources from the far past. But in reality, Croce saw, the *fascisti* were creating anew an idea or version of Rome which had never existed in the past but was developed in the present for contemporary political aims.

Croce saw history as 'philosophy in motion' and in his essay of 1893, 'History subsumed under the General Concept of Art' he argued that

> History is not a form of science, seeking to derive lawlike generalizations with predictive power, but a form of art — art, however, understood idiosyncratically, as the mode of knowledge of particulars.

Croce also anticipated many of the postmodernist theorists by denying that there was any kind of 'grand master narrative' at work. History was simply 'concrete and mundane, particular and forever incomplete.' The way to access this continuing stream of individual 'stuff', and to see some of it as a narrative bracketed off from the rest, was through the creative imagination or *fantasia*. For Croce, this use of imagination was inherent in life: through imagination we make rational sense of the world by using the tools of our cognitive and compositive faculties. Further, *what* we imagine has an effect of the world: Croce said that 'The world at every moment results from the interaction of all our efforts to impose our own form, interpretation, or truth.' What is important, however, is to remember that for Croce, historical knowing could only be 'partial, interested, and provisional,' although we can reach some particular truths as opposed to fictions.

R.G. Collingwood

The British philosopher, historiographer and historian R.G. Collingwood (*overleaf*) in *The Idea of History* (1946) further developed these ideas, stating 'the historian must re-enact the past in his own mind ... only insofar as he does this has he any historical knowledge.' This was something that Collingwood, as an archaeologist, was particularly good at, and his 1930 pamphlet, *The Philosophy of History* justified historical relativism to an unusual degree. He pointed out that every generation perceives things in the past that other generations did not. In this way, we are always – and must always be – writing history anew. It is not a static object of knowledge, but part of our own way of understanding ourselves as well as understanding the past, which we must continually undertake.

Few people would argue with Collingwood on this point; his more contentious perspective was his view of the discipline as a thought-based one. Following Croce's argument that all history was contemporary history, and Dilthey's insistence on the importance of imagination, Collingwood contended that there was a difference between 'natural processes' and 'historical processes'. The former was a process of events in time. The latter, a process of thoughts. Historians are therefore interested in the social customs and conventions which human thought has brought about. The thought is the cause of an event, and it is this that the historian seeks.

Think laterally

2. If your library has old textbooks, choose two written at least forty years apart and read about the same event in both of them. Consider how the two textbooks describe and explain the same event, and how the surrounding material situates them. Explain, in your own words, how this shows different periods writing history anew for their own time and purposes.

_____
_____
_____
_____
_____
_____

The Annales School

It was no longer clear where professional history was headed in the decades after 1918. In France the journal *Annales d'histoire economique et sociale* was founded in 1929 by Marc Bloch and Lucien Febvre at the University of Strasbourg. The journal sought to be a response to Henri Barr's observation that purely political and economic histories (or *histoire evenementielle*, as François Simiand described it) missed the mark. Instead, Bloch and Febvre argued more helpful were the study of material culture, ritual, and linguistics, using rigorous methods and data from different disciplines. As Bloch said, 'history is neither watchmaking nor cabinet construction. It is an endeavor toward better understanding.' Bloch and Febvre sought to bring social sciences as diverse as economics and sociology but also geography, psychology, anthropology and linguistics to the service of history-writing, which they characterised as 'an act of faith in the exemplary virtue of honest labour, backed by solid and conscientious research.' In terms of intellectual perspective, they confirmed medieval historian F.W. Maitland's view that one had to ask continual questions, and 'work backwards from the known to the unknown, from the certain to the uncertain.' Other members of the Annales school included the Belgian historian Henri Pirenne, who had written about medieval interactions between Christianity and Islam, and the Dutch scholar Johann Huizinga, author of *Autumn of the Middle Ages* (1919-34) and *Homo Ludens* (1938).

By drawing on evidence often neglected by purely textual study, and incorporating the methods and interpretations of different disciplines, the Annales historians produced a more complete and searching reconstruction of life in the past, particularly of groups who had added little to the textual record like the poor, women, religious minorities, and the illiterate. Bloch was executed by the Nazis for his involvement in the French Resistance, but Febvre survived the war and in 1947 became the first president of the Sixth Section of *École Pratique des Haute Études* (since 1975 known as the *École des Hautes Études en Sciences Sociales*). Under Febvre's successor Fernand Braudel (*below*), *Annales* became an internationally-regarded institution.

Braudel's massive 600,000-word work *The Mediterranean and the Mediterranean World in the Age of Philip II* (1949) showed how the physical environment affected the lives of people, particularly with regard to agriculture. Unlike the previous Annales' focus on small groups and clearly-identified events or movements, Braudel drew out the extremely slow nature of change. 'History,' he said, 'may be divided into three movements: what moves rapidly, what moves slowly and what appears not to move at all.' The way to manage this very slow sense of change, which does not respect arbitrary chronological markers such as years ending in '00', is to assume what Braudel called the *longue durée*. Most people do not recognise change during their lifetimes, and what we might regard as vital to the character of each individual – their sources of happiness, their personality, what drives them – often leaves very little trace. Nonetheless, Braudel argued, *'All history must be mobilized if one would understand the present.'* Braudel chose to present his material in a novel way – *The Mediterranean* was structured in three parts, corresponding to the layers of time which compose our perception of history. At the base, underpinning everything, is what he calls 'geohistory', the *longue durée* of environmental change. Then there is the medium-term, broader movements of economies, social structures, political events, and civilizational change which Braudel called *conjoctures*. Only above that is the fast-moving time which concerns the traditional historian. It was, Bradel showed, the job of history to uncover those long-running and impersonal forces which shape our societies and daily lives. Braudel placed very little emphasis on this last layer, or made an explicit treatment of how the three layers interacted and this naturally attracted significant criticism. But his pluralistic view of time was a vital contribution to ways of writing history and perceiving social change, and indeed, our collective existence.

Braudel's second-generation Annaliste colleague Robert Mandrou's *Introduction to Modern France* (1976) argued in favour of 'historical psychology', now more commonly termed the 'history of mentalities', as a way of correcting the perceived absence in Braudel's work of human ideas, sentiments, cultural drives, and the aspects which shaped personality. *Annales*' third generation, represented principally by Emmanuel LeRoy Ladurie, abandoned the earlier broad approach for intensive regional studies, most famously his *Montaillou: Cathars and Catholics in a French Village 1294-1324* (1975). Ladurie used sources such as church records of baptism, marriage and burial to investigate life expectancy, family size and causes of death. There was increased interest in demographic cliometrics, evident in Paul Ehrlich's bestselling *The Population Bomb* (1968).

While cliometrics was recognised as valuable tool, its shortcomings became clear because it reduced human experience to numbers; Ladurie's colleague Pierre Goubert pointed out that cliometrics obscured whether parents mourned deeply for losses or protected themselves from grief by avoiding emotional attachment to children. Cliometrics were also labour-intensive to collate and interpret and dull to read, but an interesting riposte to this criticism of cliometrics may be found in the diverse works of Niall Ferguson, originally a financial historian, who has gained an international reputation for his critical insights.

Yet even with its weaknesses and emerging divergent strands (or perhaps because of them), *Annales* has had a profound impact on historical scholarship and history writing. The scale and significance of this impact is clear in that each of the figures discussed above has become the subject of historical study.

Think laterally

3. In what ways does the Annales approach differ from Herodotus' heterogenous mix of facts and factoids about societies?

_____
_____
_____
_____
_____

Clarify

4. For your own understanding, outline the three generations of Annales' historians, and the criticisms of each one.

_____
_____
_____
_____

CONCEPT FOCUS 6: DEBATE

The importance to the discipline of a conscious, sincere, and thoughtful debate cannot be overstated. With the establishment of History as a university discipline, and the seminar as a place where historians and those in training could share ideas and identify differences, the process of debate became more prominent in historians' writing. We can think of debate as the identification of an issue, the statement of different opinions about that issue, and the alignment of participants with 'sides'. To promote and explore their perspectives, many of groups founded journals, which gave the discipline a sense of up-to-the-minute continuity, and offered a different form of writing from longer monographs.

Historical debate has flourished in the digital age, and in some ways has returned the subject to its origins, in the discussions between thinkers in the early city states. This is hardly a surprising return: the progress of an academic debate often follows a pattern of return-and-renewal. An issue reaches a point of consensus which becomes the 'orthodox' position. This is eventually challenged by a 'revisionist' position. In the back-and-forth of the two sides, a 'neo-orthodox' position may be reached, or the debate may take an entirely new trajectory.

The context of the debate will also play an important part: now that there are almost no living survivors of the First World War, the tenor of the debate about the war's origins and experience has changed – as a quick review of interviews made throughout the twentieth century shows. No historian writing about World War One today can have served in it, or even had parents who did, and this lack of proximity influences how they think and what they write about.

A good example of this is the 19th-century Sybel-Ficker debate about the relationship between Rome and the Holy Roman Empire during the Middle Ages. Although the argument happened between 1859-1861, some hundreds of years after the events in question, it was strongly influenced by a contemporary political situation: whether Austria should be part of a federal or 'Greater' Germany, or whether Austria was indeed entirely separate. Eventually, it culminated in the 1938 annexation of Austria under Nazi Germany's *Lebensraum* policy.

One place in which the debate about a particular subject is often helpfully traced is in the first chapter of a monograph or section of an article. Academic writers still tend to lay out the field and then situate their work within it, aligning themselves with one side or another, and explaining where they have made a new contribution or innovation to an existing topic. Evidence of the debate often runs throughout a work, as historians cite and quote other approaches to the same piece of evidence and then analyse deficiencies or simply differences in handling.

Read this extract from C. Behan McCullagh's article 'What do Historians Argue About?' from *History and Theory* 43.1 (2004), 18-38, p. 24. Identify where McCullagh engages in a debate, and what the different sides of the debate say.

How do historians arrive at particular facts about the past? They normally interpret observable evidence, looking for the best explanation of it in the context of what they take to have been the circumstances of its origin. In short, the interpretation of evidence depends upon their interpretation of the period in which it was created. How could their interpretation of evidence possibly provide a check upon their general interpretations of the period? We seem to have a perfect case of hermeneutical circles here: a general interpretation is supported by particular facts that in turn are supported by the general interpretation to which they contribute. The most historians could aim for, it seems, is coherence among their general and particular interpretations. It seems that there are no particular facts whose credibility is independently established, that could be used to establish the credibility of more general interpretations of which they are a part.

Several philosophers of history have presented arguments along this line, for example Berkhofer and Jenkins. In his book Beyond the Great Story, Berkhofer begins chapter three ("Historical Representations and Truthfulness") by asking "are some interpretations better than most or all others?" He points out that "normal historians" believe interpretations should be constrained by the facts they infer from evidence. He then remarks: "The problem with historical facts, as with histories themselves, is that they are constructions and interpretations of the past. Evidence is not fact until given meaning in accordance with some framework or perspective." He adds: "Thus interpretation plays a much larger role in normal history than the profession likes to admit." At the end of this chapter Berkhofer describes how historians decide the truth of their descriptions of the past, Historians interpret the evidence available to them in the context of other historical texts they have read, and their general knowledge of the world. "Readers' politics and ethics, like their disciplinary paradigms and belief systems, all operate as determinants of historical truthfulness," he says.

Normal historians, as Berkhofer is aware, produce arguments in defense of their interpretations of evidence. But Berkhofer dismisses such arguments as nothing other than rhetorical devices: "modern rhetorical analysis, as it did classically, treats both the logic and the stylistics of argument as parts of a presentation meant to persuade its hearers or readers.'" Indeed, he accepts as an implication of his position that truth and ideology cannot easily be distinguished, and queries the need to judge interpretations on cognitive rather than moral or aesthetic grounds.

Jenkins has produced a similar argument in his Introduction to The Postmodern History Reader. He writes, "The facts cannot themselves indicate their significance as though it were inherent in them. To give significance to the facts an external theory of significance is aways needed." Indeed, he goes on, the facts that historians refer to "are constituted through the processes of representation" and so cannot possibly act as a check upon such representations. Jenkins emphasizes the implication of his argument for traditional history: it lacks the empirical foundation which it was once assumed to have. He writes of modernist history as "a self-referential, problematical expression of interests, an ideological-interpretative discourse without any non-historicized access to the past as such. In fact history now appears to be just one more foundationless, positioned expression in a world of foundationless, positioned expressions."

Those who present arguments like these make two important assumptions both of which are false. The first is that the credibility of the particular facts upon which which general interpretations depend is always a function of the credibility of those interpretations. The truth is that the credibility of description of particular historical facts is often, indeed normally, though not always, independent of the credibility of the general interpretations they support. They ignore the fact that many interpretations of observable evidence, many statements of particular historical facts, are so strongly supported as to be virtually certain. These provide excellent independent support for general interpretations that rest upon them.

English-language social historians

Anglophone historians in the post-war era also focused on social history, with the journal *Past and Present* (1952) bringing together left-wing historians like Christopher Hill, Eric Hobsbawm, and E.P. Thompson and non-Marxists like R.H. Tawney and Lawrence Stone. Thompson's *Making of the English Working Class* (1963) contrasted sharply with mainstream conventional histories of the Industrial Revolution by rejecting the view that working-class suffering was the unavoidable cost of technological and economic progress. Although each of these historians made a significant impact on the reading public, they were building on the work of Fabians like Sidney and Beatrice Webb whose books on trade unionism, the Co-operative Movement, and 'Industrial democracy' had sought to establish the facts upon which social reform could occur.

Thompson studied how religion, particularly 'low church' and dissenting traditions, shaped working-class consciousness and expressions of culture and values. He asserted that working class people were not simply controlled by an externally-imposed religion, but chose and shaped religious views and expression for themselves. As part of this new way of looking at the nexus of class and religion Thompson contributed a new defintion of class. Instead of a stratum in a hierarchy which encompassed all of society, class was an experience, 'largely determined by the productive relations into which men are born – or enter involuntarily.' Class, he wrote, 'happens'. It is not a fixed quality, but the product of an event in which different people participate and articulate the identity of their interests as between themselves, and against interests that are different from (and usually opposed to) theirs. This was a highly original way of looking at what class was, and where we can expect to find evidence of it in the record. Thompson's massive book continues to be prescribed to undergraduate students.

Think laterally

5. For your own understanding, outline the ways in which 'social' history differs from political history. This will require a definition of *society* and *politics*.

The Modern Skeptics

Two decades after the end of the Second World War, then, history-writing was recognised as an established part of public life. While not primarily a quantitative social science like economics or politics, history could and did express the entire spectrum of opinions and methodologies in public (particularly political) life. In the early and middle years of the twentieth century, an approach and general mindset had gradually emerged in Anglophone historians which Arthur Marwick has called 'modern empiricism'. It can be characterized by a common-sense resistance to dogmatic theorizing and pattern-seeking, and a distrust of generalization and overtly political affiliation. In this respect, such historians are the antithesis of the British Marxists described above. The modern empirical, or skeptical, perspective accepts the importance of abrupt change and the causes of this in unpredictable and even irrational events. While unwilling to rewrite history to suit contemporary political fads, this perspective also accepts that much of what is written is contingent on available facts and perspectives and may need to be revised for further accuracy and fairness, as well as relevance to the reading public. While quantification is germane to some types of source-material, the entire venture of historical narrative cannot be boiled down to quantifications, nor should it. Historians as personally and politically disparate as George Kitson Clark, G.R. Elton, A.J.P. Taylor, and even Hugh Trevor-Roper have been placed in this group.

In 1961 E.H. Carr published the G.M. Trevelyan Lectures in a book called *What is History?* This book called into question the notion of historical objectivity. Carr pointed out that historians tended to select areas of focus because they interested *them* and not necessarily because they were 'all that was left' to study. These areas of focus, written up to support a historical hypothesis, were easily mistaken for the totality of knowledge about that period of history by readers. Carr returned to Carl Becker's earlier argument about the subjective nature of historical knowledge, urging students to 'study the historian before you study his facts.' Clearly, the historical profession felt Carr's work important enough to commemorate on its fortieth anniversary with another publication called *What is History Now?* Where contemporary historians provided new answers to Carr's question. An excellent example of a historian whose personal and cultural affiliations significantly influenced his historical method was Lewis Namier, about whom there is more in **Concept Focus 7: The Historian Themselves.**

Having the critical lens of their own students turned upon them did not sit well with historians who believed that their own lives and the material they studied were separate things. G.R. Elton's *The Practice of History* (1967) and J.H. Hexter's *The History Primer*, *Doing History* and *On Historians: Reappraisals of the Masters of Modern History* voiced the orthodox view that 'evidence and proof are never radical or conservative,' and refused to engage with the idea that such items were, ipso facto, constructed by a historian who stood in the stream of history and was thus possessed of a perspective which left its mark on his work.

Think laterally

In this troubled time we can still see historians and historiographers responding *to* each other – that is, we see the beginning of a conversation between historians and groups of historians, as they work through what history-writing is and how to go about it.

6. How is this the case for the twentieth century historiographers you have read about in this chapter?

Clarify

7. How do the approaches of 20th century historians differ from historians of previous periods? You can choose two or three previous historians or periods to comment on, if you want to be more specific.

Reading task 6

Read the following passage.

Let us take a look at the process by which a mere fact about the past is transformed into a fact of history. At Stalybridge Wakes in 1850, a vendor of gingerbread, as the result of some petty dispute, was deliberately kicked to death by an angry mob. Is this a fact of history? A year ago I should unhesitatingly have said 'no'. It was recorded by an eye-witness in some little-known memoirs; but I had never seen it judged worthy of mention by any historian. A year ago Dr Kitson Clark cited it in his Ford lectures in Oxford. Does this make it into a historical fact? Not, I think, yet. Its present status, I suggest, is that it has been proposed for membership of the select club of historical facts. It now awaits a seconder and sponsors. It may be that in the course of the next few years we shall see this fact appearing first in footnotes, then in the text, of articles and books about nineteenth-century England, and that in twenty or thirty years' time it may be a well-established historical fact. Alternatively, nobody may take it up, in which case it will relapse into the limbo of unhistorical facts about the past from which Dr Kitson Clark has gallantly attempted to rescue it. What will decide which of these two things will happen? It will depend, I think, on whether the thesis or interpretation in support of which Dr Kitson Clark cited this incident is accepted by other historians as valid and significant. Its status as a historical fact will turn on a question of interpretation. This element of interpretation enters into every fact of history.

1. In your own words, explain what the writer regards as the difference between a fact and a fact of history.

2. Do you agree with the writer? Give an example from your own knowledge which supports your answer.

3. Based on what you have read in this chapter, who do you think the writer is? Justify your answer.

4. Identify another historiographer or historiographical school to which this extract responds, either by supporting or refuting the writer's ideas. (If you've correctly identified the writer, you should be able to locate the rest of the work in your library, where he responds to several other historians by name).

Chapter revision statement

Write a list of the key points from this chapter.

_____
_____
_____
_____
_____
_____
_____
_____
_____
_____

Use the list to write a short statement about important features in the discipline of History during the period studied in this chapter.

_____
_____
_____
_____
_____
_____
_____
_____

Notes

_____
_____
_____
_____
_____
_____
_____

Chapter 7: Wars in the Academy

During the second half of the 20th century the place that History had achieved in culture and academic life faced challenges from at least three sources. The historiographer Jeremy Popkin observes that the emerging generation adopted a conflict-dominated perspective from which they wrote and assessed history. In Popkin's explanation, the dominant features of the post-1945 generation of historians were the Cold War, the civil rights campaigns and the Vietnam war.

The widespread student protests in the mid-1960s signalled that the baby boomers were increasingly willing to challenge orthodox views about how the world worked. The October 1962 Cuban missile crisis was a hiatus from which the generation born immediately prior to, and during, the Second World War reflected on conflict. French protests over the recognition of Algeria, years after other European colonial powers had recognized their own newly-independent ex-colonies, culminated in a 1968 general strike that almost toppled the government.

Clarify

1. By defining this group of conflict-centered historians by the date of their birth, what strain of historiographical thinking is Popkin following?

While the activities of some historians in the west, for example the *Past and Present* group's E.P. Thompson and Eric Hobsbawm, had anticipated the emerging demands for 'revisionist' history, the 1960s went further, particularly in North American universities, where several historians came to view the established historical methods of the Rankean tradition as 'devices for stifling subversive questions and maintaining traditional structures of authority.'

In the spirit of 'grassroots change' undergraduate students began to demand new courses that spoke directly to their own concerns, such as explanations for the Vietnam War, radical movements in the past, and inconsistencies with liberal progress like the status of minorities in the United States. Broadly speaking, the historians who taught these courses can be grouped together under the named 'New Left', or new social history, although the New Left covers many more thinkers than just historians.

Louise A. Tilly, one of the most widely-read social historians, characterised social history as documenting large structural changes, reconstructing the lives of ordinary people during those changes, and connecting the two things. Tilly and her husband, Charles Tilly, wrote several books which broke new ground on the factors shaping family life over the course of the modern age. *Women, Work, and Family* presented a comprehensive analysis of women's wage-labour and the systemic inequalities of which it was part.

In some universities teachers and students worked together to construct courses that responded to student interest and questions, and were innovative in the way that history was taught in tertiary settings: Raphael Samuel's 'History Workshop' (1967) and Natalie Zemon Davis and Jill Ker Conway's women's history course in Toronto (1971) combined the input of students, teachers, and workers in an attempt to bring History out of the ivory tower and into the lives of ordinary men and women.

Conservative academics protested that these teaching experiments appeared to devalue the stringency of historical method and their own hard-won knowledge of (sometimes arcane) period-based history. In *Historians' Fallacies* (1970) David Hackett Fischer argued that much of the work done in this period was not 'serious', and often betrayed muddled thinking:

> Many pundits today are in the habit of misquoting Santayana's epigram, *Those who cannot remember the past are condemned to repeat it.* Maybe some people have come to grief this way, but they are probably fewer than those who have fallen into the opposite error. *One is apt to perish in politics from too much memory,* Tocqueville wrote somewhere, with equal truth and greater insight.

Hackett nonetheless failed to reduce the enthusiasm, or the perceived need, for new approaches. Taking the long perspective, Popkin concludes that:

> In some ways these debates can be read as renewals of older controversies; one can imagine Herodotus taking the side of today's optimists and Thucydides warning against the hazards of innovation. In other ways, however, the issues that divide historians today are really new and require new responses.

Think laterally

It could be argued that this discussion shows that History had finally come into its own as a discipline because it was now fighting to protect its own authority.

2. What does 'authority' mean to you in terms of History as a discipline? How does this permit the participation of non-academic people and non-academic ways of expressing historical consciousness?

_____
_____
_____
_____
_____

ISBN 9780645591422

What lay behind these sudden tectonic shifts in a discipline which had secured its place in the academy, produced a valuable social contribution, and now amassed a body of work fundamentally different from other styles of knowing, thinking, and writing? The answer lay partly in the work of the Francophone trio of Paul Ricoeur (1913-2005), Jean-François Lyotard (1924-1998) and Michel Foucault (1926-1984). These men (and others in Europe and, to a limited extent, the United States), are termed postmodernists and poststructuralists, because their work emphasised the loss of faith in grand narratives of progress and Enlightenment rationality, and the systematic dismantling of texts which promoted those claims.

In retrospect it seems easy to understand how such disillusionment could arise from the industrial-scale murder of two World Wars, and the failings of the cultural narratives and political machinery which allowed those wars to occur. Such ideals as 'Man and Progress' and 'The Transparency of Truth' had blinded people, including (and perhaps especially) academics, to the fact that no such things existed. They were fictions, dead metaphors, products of texts which only existed as long as someone was reading them. They had no 'real' existence at all. Michel Foucault (*left*) sought to explode the authority of academic history, by showing that the seamless course of history, leading from one significant event to another, was an illusion. All that really existed was a continual struggle. If history had any value, it was showing what illusions and deceptions were being perpetrated in the present – mostly by those at the top of power-structures such as universities, prisons, hospitals, and schools. Even the language of History was part of the illusion. Written history was just a series of statements which historians swapped, manipulated, and kept as cultural capital for themselves. This patchwork of statements had nothing to do with the past, except in mutilating it. Scientific knowledge (in the sense of knowledge built on a rational or empirical foundation) was linked to the exercise of power: those who knew how to 'use' rationality wielded power, those who didn't were disempowered by virtue of being 'irrational' or 'emotional'.

Although many of Foucault's own historical works have been criticised for their partiality, lop-sided use of data, and libertarian-anarchist agenda, they performed an important service in reminding society at large that other ways of thinking existed, and had been progressively devalued by a cultural hegemony which gave power to a very small number of people. This power was vested in 'discourse', or ways of talking, thinking, and representing. Discourse analysis was therefore a powerful, though not always welcome, tool for many disciplines.

More broadly, the work of postmodernists showed the dark tendencies of certain foundational narratives of the West: Man, Civilization, Narrative, and Democracy were all narratives about what was good, necessary, superior, and justified. Anything else was Other and inferior: individual people (including women), 'un-civilization', non-narrative, and non-democratic, had all been positioned as objects which were viewed within a largely male, white, European, liberal-individualist tradition. The result of this revelation was that such groups asserted their own right and need to 'do' History. Women's history, the histories of colonized peoples, of working-class people, and even of non-people – the planet, animals, periods other than those of our species – have all come about because of postmodernism.

CONCEPT FOCUS 7: THE HISTORIAN THEMSELVES

E.H. Carr's dictum to study the historian before you study their facts caused serious consternation in the discipline, but it is really common sense. Knowing that, for example, G.M. Trevelyan had served as an ambulance driver during the First World War, and had been dismayed by the chaos and horrors of 'industrial warfare' helps us to understand possible reasons behind his moderation of a Whig narrative of progress based on rationality and technology. Similarly, knowing that Ibn Khaldun had been the subject of scurrilous gossip which had eventually cost him his place at court in part explains his awareness that historians should be skeptical in their search for causes and rigorous in their standards of evidence. Although an individual's personal background does not necessarily entail their intellectual perspective, it is very likely to contribute to it. What they regard as valuable, significant, truthful, and causative is often shaped by the life they have lived.

A good example of a historian whose family, political, and intellectual background may have influenced their writing was Lewis Namier (born Ludwik Bernstein Niemirowski 1888-1960). Namier developed a method of exhaustive biography which he applied to the study of the British parliament – he wrote a history of the institution by means of a vast network of inter-related biographies of its members, through which he tested certain long-held historical views about the nature of a period, the causes of events, and ideas which arose during them. The Namier Method, or prosopography, has since been criticised for its narrow structuralism, but it was at one time practically *de rigeur* for historians.

Namier's general pessimism about human motives and the possibility of self-awareness leading to self-determination, is very apparent in his histories.

Read the following quotations from different works by Namier. Then read one of the articles from the list, and explain about how Namier's biography provides insight into how he may have arrived at these ideas.

1. The subject matter of history is human affairs, men in action, things which have happened and how they happened; concrete events fixed in time and space, and their grounding in the thoughts and feelings of men – not things universal and generalized; events as complex and diversified as the men who wrought them, those rational beings who knowledge is seldom sufficient, whose ideas are but distantly related to reality, and who are never moved by reason alone.

2. …whatever theories of "free will" theologians and philosophers may develop with regard to the individual, there can be no free will in the thinking and actions of the masses, any more than in the revolutions of planets, in the migrations of birds, and in the plunging of hordes of lemmings into the sea.

3. There is some well-nigh mystical power in the ownership of spaces — for it is not the command of resources alone which makes the strength of the landowner, but that he has a place in the world which he can call his own, from which he can ward off strangers, and in which he himself is rooted — the superiority of a tree to a log.

4. One would expect people to remember the past and to imagine the future. But in fact, when discoursing or writing about history, they imagine it in terms of their own experience, and when trying to gauge the future they cite supposed analogies from the past: till, by a double process of repetition, they imagine the past and remember the future.

John Brooke, 'Namier and Namierism,' *History and Theory* 3.3 (1964), 331-347.

https://www.jstor.org/stable/2504236

D.W. Hayton, 'Lewis Namier: Nationality, Territory and Zionism,' *International Journal of Politics, Culture, and Society* 30.2 Special Issue: *Jewish Conditions, Theories of Nationalism* (June 2017), 171-82.

https://www.jstor.org/stable/48720420

J.L. Talmon, 'The Ordeal of Sir Lewis Namier: The Man, the Historian, the Jew,' *Commentary* March (1962), https://www.commentary.org/articles/j-talmon/the-ordeal-of-sir-lewis-namier-the-man-the-historian-the-jew/

The History of Women and Women in History

As Louise A. Tilly's study of women and work showed, the historical experience of a large group which was rarely represented in historical writing was one area of historical study that badly needed revised. If the campaigners for women's suffrage from around 1890-1918 were the 'first wave' of feminists, the 'second wave' covered the period around 1960-1990. The idea that female life was, or should be, was contained in the un- or de-historicized space of the home had been on hiatus during the war while women's labour was badly needed. When it returned in force after the Second World War, Simon de Beauvoir's *The Second Sex* (1949) and Betty Friedan's *The Feminine Mystique* (1963) challenged it stringently.

Adopting Thomas S. Kuhn's model of the development of science and scientific revolutions, Gerda Lerner (*left*) posited that the emerging movement of women's history represented a 'paradigm shift' in the discipline. Lerner and her colleagues demanded that two connected areas be reconsidered: one was the experience of women in the historical past; the second was the experience of women who researched and taught about that historical past. Even if researchers were reconsidering those excluded from positions of power, and mostly absent from political and military history, the gendered perspective of usually male researchers was simply another way in which history would continue to dispossess and deny the presence of women. The presence and experience of women in the past should, female historians now argued, be researched more deeply and written about more equitably. There should therefore be more female historians in the discipline.

The website of the Berkshire Conference of Women Historians. Institutional – and individual – websites are instructive of a historian or group's self-presentation and attitude to technology and public access.

In 1969 the Coordinating Committee on Women in the Historical Profession was formed to address the inequalities present in the American Historical Association, which Bernice Carroll characterized as 'a gentlemen's protection society . . . openly supporting practices of sexism, racism, classism, heterosexism, and antisemitism.' The Committee pressed the AHA to review the lack of inclusion of women both within its own ranks and within leading universities. The resulting Berkshire Conference on Women in History was launched in 1973. Known as 'The Big Berks', the triennial conference is now the largest gathering of women historians in the world.

It is important to remember, however, that there is as much diversity of subject matter, historical method, and political opinion among female historians as there is among male. Yet the perception that women are still marginalized in both history, historiography, and the teaching of history, is substantial enough to justify continued conferences, courses, and journals which deal purely with these problems.

Paradigm shifts

Historians' willingness to reframe questions and perspectives was increased by Thomas Kuhn's *The Structure of Scientific Revolutions* (1962). Perhaps to justify the existence of scientific societies and the model of science as a group pursuit, the western concept of scientific knowledge had for a long time been one of gradual and communal increase. Rather like the Darwinian model of evolution as a process of continual adaptation to changing surroundings and survival-demands, the outsider might not notice from one decade to the next how scientific knowledge had 'progressed' unless they were watching it in tiny increments. Kuhn pointed out that some of the most important 'paradigm-changing' moments in scientific thinking had not been gradual, but rather had come about in sudden jumps. The Newtonian vision of the mechanical universe and Einstein's theory of relativity were both the result of sudden total changes in the way individual scientists conceptualised a problem and solved it. There might not, he said, be a single criterion of truth for the discipline of History, and accepting this would mean a step-change or paradigm shift in the way we think.

Could the same sudden, individually-driven paradigm-change happen in historiography? The Rankean model of History as a discipline with a specialized skill-set, performed only by people who had trained in that discipline and handed on within an exclusive academic culture (however much they may condescend to involve outsiders) seemed very similar to the way science and scientific problems had been viewed. It was a system, structured and powered by the consensus of those involved, and which had a vested interest (like all systems) in not changing itself. With the publication of Kuhn's work, many disciplines reconsidered their own criteria for 'truth' and asked whether they were indeed open to what Kuhn termed 'paradigm shift.' That Kuhn's work was republished in a fiftieth anniversary edition is compelling evidence of its singular importance.

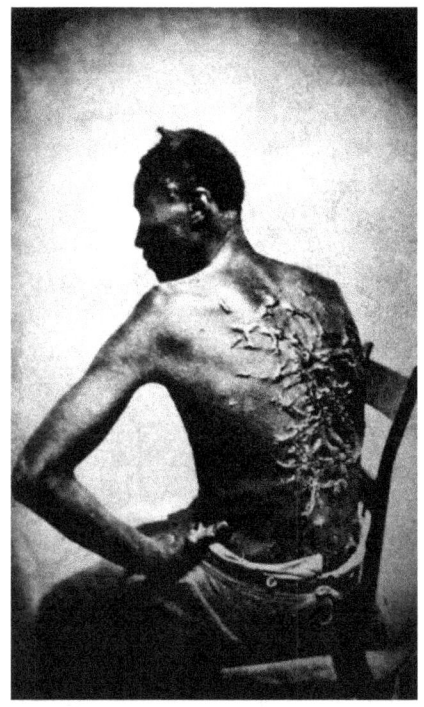

One highly controversial example of a paradigm-shift came in 1974 with the publication of Robert Fogel and Stanley Engerman's *Time on the Cross: The Economics of American Negro Slavery*. It remains fundamental to many parts of modern America to regard every aspect of antebellum slavery as exemplifying cruelty and trauma. But Fogel and Engerman threatened this blanket belief with the conclusions drawn from their quantitative survey of physical punishment. They suggested that in fact whipping was relatively infrequent, and that slaves generally affirmed the value of hard work impressed on them by their owners because slavery was an 'economically viable institution' which had some benefits for the slaves themselves. Accepting that their thesis was likely to be controversial, both authors said that their aim was to challenge myths about African Americans which had arisen as a result of the slavery debate, and to correct inaccuracies about the economic viability of slavery as an institution.

Nevertheless, the outcry which resulted was directed at both the method and the conclusions drawn from it. Critics argued that Fogel and Engerman had used small, possibly unrepresentative, samples of data. Within a year, Herbert Gutman's *Slavery and the Numbers Game* challenged Fogel and Engerman's conclusions, arguing that they had used insufficient measurements. Gutman also queried whether slaves really had internalized the 'Protestant work ethic'. If they had, he suggested, the system of rewards and punishments would support this – but it did not seem to. Other, non-cliometric, historians of slavery said that such data could not represent the enslaved condition. The resulting controversy witnessed History, in company with other humanities and social sciences, being swept into debate with advocates of the so-called 'linguistic' and 'cultural' turns.

Think laterally

3. Read the 'Coherence theory of truth' in Wikipedia. How does Kuhn's argument that there might not be a single criterion for historical truth fit the coherence theory? Which theory of truth that you've come across so far opposes the coherence theory?

The Cultural and Linguistic Turns

In 1973 the anthropologist Clifford Geertz, who is remembered for his focus on cultural symbols, had argued that language was the key to comprehending human experiences. Rather than seeing History as a narrative of events in search of 'truth', Geertz suggested that the analysis of culture was an interpretation of events in search of meaning. Even more importantly, he argued that 'Meaning is socially, historically, and rhetorically constructed.'

The focus on meaning was the result of the twentieth-century's greater interest in real people's lived experience, rather than the sociological or geo-political 'laws' which governed large groups likenations. The 'cultural turn' now suggested that what mattered to people in the past and how they had made it apparent was just as worthy of historical study as what happened and why it had come about.

That historians faced a paradigm shift in Kuhn's sense became evident in the heated controversy caused by Hayden White's *Metahistory: The Historical Imagination in 19th-century Europe* (1973), probably the single most controversial work of historiography in the late twentieth-century. Essentially, White *(left)* said, there was no real difference between a work of literature and a work of history:

> Readers of histories and novels can hardly fail to be struck by their similarities. There are many histories that could pass for novels, and many novels that could pass for histories, considered in purely formal (or, I should say, formalist) terms. Viewed simply as verbal artefacts, histories and novels are indistinguishable from one another. We cannot easily distinguish between them on formal grounds unless we approach them with specific preconceptions about the kinds of truths that each is supposed to deal in. But the aim of the writer of a novel must be the same as that of the writer of a history.

White used the literary theory of Northrop Frye to examine how historians had written their material and argued that, while historians may have been following factual source material, they had to choose a *way* to write it up which followed the literary forms of comedy, tragedy, romance and so on. White used the term 'emplotment' to suggest that, far from transparently reflecting or reporting on the past, historians were actually writing down their own perception of the events. Just as one person might write the story of Marie Antoinette as a sit-com, another might see it as a classical tragedy, and another as a teen drama.

Historians reacted with some consternation to his claim that

> I will consider the historical work as what it most manifestly is - that is to say, a verbal structure in the form of a narrative prose discourse that purports to be a model, or an icon, of past structures and processes in the interests of explaining what they were by representing them.

Even reviewers who liked the book recognized the damage it could do to the profession; G.R. Elton suggested that White's was 'the most damaging undertaking ever performed by an historian on his profession.' The issues that *Metahistory* raised became the focus of historiographical debate during the late twentieth century and still impact upon the present. White's view of the literary character of historians' narratives has certainly made historians aware of the perception of their work and the presence of 'unscrupulous' theorists.

Think laterally

4. Do you think that White's argument merited the furore it caused? What might have been behind this dislike of being mistaken for creators of literature by those who rejected White's argument?

In one way or another, many of these historians were performing discourse analysis, showing how discourse – the way we talk about things, and the differing degrees of power vested in discourses – was a very powerful element of social control. Foucault's *Madness and Civilisation* (1961), for example, had argued that insanity was culturally constructed by the grand narrative of Rationality is Best, and that language determined the difference between 'mad', 'visionary', and 'blessed'. Grand Narratives, to use Lyotard's term, made people think that the past was 'out there' and somehow separate to the words which transparently represented it. Foucault showed that we constructed the past and our perspective on it through the language that we used, and that the external quality of the past was very much an illusion of discourse. The medieval anchoress Julian of Norwich who had visions – or delusions, depending on the type of discourse you use – could be seen as a rare and gifted individual who had spiritual experiences well outside the range of normal people, and described them in prose of unusual insight and fluency. But in a different discourse, she was a delusional schizophrenic who was of academic interest because of her rambling and unconstrained prose, and who showed that medieval society valued religious experience so highly that it could not or would not distinguish mental illness from genuinely unexplained phenomenon. In the former case, Julian of Norwich was worthy of veneration and emulation. In the latter, she is an object of pity and condemnation. In *Discipline and Punish* (1975) Foucault extended his argument about the power of discourse to historians themselves, reminding readers that

> There is no power relation without the correlative constitution of a field of knowledge, nor any knowledge that does not presuppose and constitute at the same time power relations.

In other words, by claiming that something constitutes 'knowledge', historians were making claims to their own power and authority as articulators and curators of that knowledge. Like White, Geertz and Kuhn, the writing of interdisciplinary theorists from the postmodern school can sometimes seem obscure and even Jungian, but it reveals the power-plays and politics which lay behind, and was present in, writing – particularly academic writing.

Think laterally

5. As an illustration of Foucault's point, think about things which society once found unmentionable: cancer; childbirth; bankruptcy; AIDS; depression; homosexuality, cohabitation without marriage. Such subjects were either avoided or 'talked around'. Take one from the list and write the euphemisms or expressions used to refer to this in a socially-acceptable way.

_____
_____
_____
_____
_____
_____
_____
_____

6. How does our society continue to promote the idea that language and the thing it talks about, are different? In what ways do people fight back against this, both in everyday life and in academic writing?

_____
_____
_____
_____
_____
_____
_____
_____

 Overlapping the later work of White and Foucault, Jean François Lyotard's *The Post-Modern Condition* (1979) argued that the growth of technology and thus our ability to control things more precisely now meant that people did not need the grand narratives which sought to explain everything by a very general, falsely grandiose, story. Smaller, more individual narratives could explain social change and political problems. However, Lyotard (*left*) also noted the effect of the failure of grand narratives on disciplines as diverse as science and history: without the lofty 'reasons why', disciplines had to find new ways of legitimating themselves. Lyotard was fundamentally pessimistic about this and predicted that we would turn increasingly to information science and artificial intelligence. The human drive for meaning was, he claimed, ultimately doomed to lose faith in itself even as the human capacity for production increased. The grand narrative of emancipation through greater technological control had foundered on the realities of greater technological prowess. One way in which Lyotard was remarkably prescient was his recognition of the commodification of information:

> Knowledge in the form of an informational commodity indispensable to productive power is already, and will continue to be, a major- perhaps the major – stake in the world-wide competition for power. It is conceivable the nation state will one day fight for control of information, just as they battled over territory, and afterwards for control of access to and exploitation of raw materials and cheap labor. A new field opened for industrial and commercial strategies on the one hand, and political and military strategies.

Think laterally

7. For your own understanding, paraphrase Lyotard's argument. You will need a clear grasp of what a 'grand narrative' is.

___

___

___

Paul Ricoeur's *Time and Narrative* (1984) tried to incorporate Hayden White's insights into the nature of history while maintaining the distinction between history and fiction. The importance of narrative, he argued, lay in its ability to represent how we experience time – both cosmological time, and phenomenological time. Our sense of understanding always deals with time in some way, and the main way is through a narrative which is intrinsically anchored in time. Fiction, however, is different to historical narrative. Evidence outside the historical narrative can be dated, that is, placed in both cosmological and phenomenological time. Fiction is not constrained by this.

An important difference between Ricoeur and other post-structuralists like Foucault and Derrida is that Ricoeur saw subjectivity as existing in the body and the material world. This means that our sense of things, including ourselves, is tied to the real world and things in it –

Derrida and Foucault thought that our sense of subjectivity was simply a product of language (language speaking language through language, if you like). What Ricoeur's view also entailed was the idea that our experience of the world and our view of ourselves would also change according to the time in which we lived – because the physical world which informed us was different.

Many critics, especially Anglophone ones, have seen the works of Foucault, Lyotard and Ricoeur as abstruse French post-modernist theories from the disrupted period after 1968. The French theorists might produce good explanations of how important language was to the meaning conveyed by it, but they could not explain how some things happened in a pre- or extra-linguistic sense, such as historical change. Because they focused on language in its many guises, they also treated institutions such as governments simply as products and producers of language – they were language-control machines, in other words. This was just as impersonal and imprecise as the grand-narratives which they criticized.

However, Christopher Clark's *Sleepwalkers* (2013), and Clark's post-publication discussions of this work as a device to break the stalemate in historical literature about the origins of the First World War, are persuasive evidence of Hayden White's positive influence on history-writing. That Clark's work has been well-received and recognised is evidenced in his appointment as Regius Professor of History at Cambridge and his knighthood.

Think laterally

8. What assumption about History's core function is made by critics of the cultural turn?

Never have historians had so much evidence at their disposal; never has there been so much mistrust about what the evidence shows. How do the multiple pieces of the past cohere? What is the common thread linking literary texts, religious art, popular songs, marriage customs, and farm implements? That human beings created all these things may not be enough to confer an integrated meaning on clues that are not clearly linked or on witnesses of uncertain authority. This difficulty is particularly characteristic of the realm of values, beliefs, and attitudes — culture in the broadest sense ... The desire to push history to the very edge of documentary evidence has produced both exhilarating vistas and a significant unease at the prospect that the ground where historians stand, gazing into the past may suddenly give way. On the one hand ... historians currently enjoy a bracing sense of adventure; on the other, they are struggling to impose coherence on what threatens at times to become nothing more than a ... tale.

9. Do you agree with James Wilkerson about this? What has your reading about history-writing in the 20th century made you think about this?

ISBN 9780645591422

Reading task 7

Read the following passage, from Hayden White's article 'Historicism, History, and the Figurative Imagination', *History and Theory*, Vol 14, No 4, Beheift 14: *Essays on Historicism* (Dec. 1975), 48-67.

I have argued elsewhere that an historical discourse should not be regarded as a mirror image of the set of events that it claims simply to describe. On the contrary, the historical discourse should be viewed as a sign-system which points in two directions simultaneously: first, toward the set of events it purports to describe and, second, toward the generic story form, to which it tacitly likens the set in order to disclose its formal coherence considered as either a structure or a process. Thus, for example, a given set of events, arranged more or less chronologically, but encoded so as to appear as phases of a process with a discernible beginning, middle, and end, may be emplotted as a Romance, Comedy, Tragedy, Epic, or what have you, depending upon the valences assigned to different events in the series as elements of recognizable archetypal story-forms. (p.54)

Use the digital library JSTOR to find the rest of this article and read the pp.53-55. You should have access to JSTOR through your school, local, or state library; you will need it for the long essay.

1. Explain the difference between 'historical' and 'historicist' thinking on which White comments.

_____

2. Clarify (in simpler language) the relationship between 'the different types of historical discourse' and 'the modalities of figurative language-use'.

_____

3. Why might G.R. Elton have thought this idea 'dangerous'?

4. Give an example of a piece of History-writing which seems to follow a particular emplotment such as Romance or Tragedy.

5. Do you agree with White that History is basically just a form of literature, and should be studied as such?

6. The journal *History and Theory* was founded in 1960. All of its back-issues can be read in JSTOR. Compare how history students access this journal with how contemporary readers of Gibbon's *History of the Decline and Fall of the Roman Empire* (published 1776-1789) read his work. What might be the effect for historical debate?

ISBN 9780645591422

Chapter revision statement

Write a list of the key points from this chapter.

_____
_____
_____
_____
_____
_____
_____
_____
_____
_____

Use the list to write a short statement about important features in the discipline of History during the period studied in this chapter.

_____
_____
_____
_____
_____
_____
_____
_____

Notes

_____
_____
_____
_____
_____
_____
_____
_____
_____

Chapter 8: Recent times 1 – history or histories?

Questions remain about the impact of the cultural turn and about how and why history is written, but there can be no question that it has significantly influenced *who* does history and *what* history is produced. The result has been the emergence of new 'genres' of history-writing.

Post-Colonial Perspectives

Despite the many paradigm shifts of the last fifty years, for most people the study of history still means a narrative of the antecedents to the modern, western, nation state, focused mainly on the upper echelons. Although some aspects – particularly the nation state, and its powerful classes – were challenged after the Second World War, historians still relied on a western focus and a western definition of modernity. Europe was still the centre; other nations and cultures were peripheral. Europe (and the United States as the fullest articulation of westernism) still determined the shape and structure of historical thinking, the 'us' against which other cultures were an excluded or suppressed 'them'.

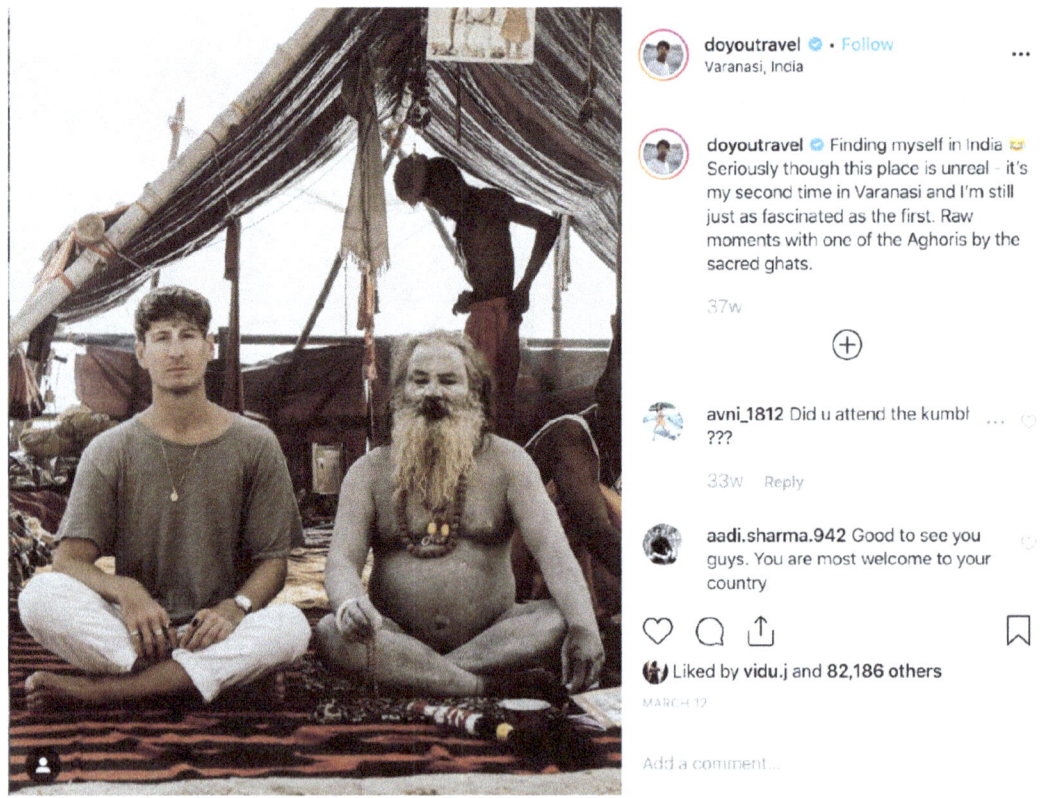

Said's Orientalism *pointed out how western artists and writers 'cherry-picked' elements of the east from North Africa to Japan in order to depict them as exotic, primitive, and ungoverned – and to justify their co-option by western powers. The idea of the exotic east is still alive and well in the digital space.*

This 'binary social relation' of Occident and Orient was theorized in *Orientalism* (1978), the literary critic Edward Said's book about how the West saw the East (which he defined very broadly indeed). Said argued that western colonial and imperial projects had denied eastern cultures a history, progress, and political technology of their own. An entrenched binarism meant that neither east nor west could exist independently of the other: the west's view of itself as the provider of rational, civilized progress, technology, and developed culture required the existence of a backward, irrational and un(der)developed group upon which to focus its power.

> To the extent that Western scholars were aware of contemporary Orientals or Oriental movements of thought and culture, these were perceived either as silent shadows to be animated by the Orientalist, brought into reality by them, or as a kind of cultural and international proletariat useful for the Orientalist's grander interpretive activity.

To exist in any academically meaningful way, that is, by having its past and culture written down and made the subject of study, the east had to have access to the west, which would provide the technology by which they were commemorated and studied.

Critics pointed out some serious flaws in Said's work. One was his own 'orientalist' approach, of grouping together hundreds of different cultural groups whose only similarity had been contact with European colonial powers. He implied that Orientalism was a 'style of thought' and a 'corporate institution' for dealing with the west, but his evidence came from disparate texts and times, and ignored the many European scholars who had engaged knowledgeably and humbly with the histories, languages, and cultures of Asia.

One important factor which Said raised in his critique of Western historians' disregard of non-western cultures was that many other cultures have their own modes of historical action, consciousness, and record. Many non-literate societies and cultures in Africa, the Pacific, and Australia, have a substantial sense of history, but produce no written sources. Even highly literate cultures do not create records of some elements of their own societies – as the lack of historical records for the lowest castes in Indian and Japan shows.

Dipesh Chakrabarty's *Provincialising Europe: Postcolonial Thought and Historical Differences* (2000) argues that historicist thinking

> enabled European domination of the world in the 19th-century ... Historicism is what made modern vanity or capitalism look not simply global but rather as something that became global over time by originating in one place (Europe) and then spreading outside it.

Chakrabarty's work focuses on revealing the mechanisms by which Eurocentric historians have made claims to power and knowledge in their writing. They have done this by positioning the European historical method as normative, he argues, and so forcing every other type of history into a 'subaltern' position. They must acknowledge and respond to western norms, thereby colluding in their own marginalisation. The mission of Subaltern Studies is therefore 'to write into the history of modernity the ambivalences, contradictions, use of force and the tragedies and ironies that attend it.' Dipesh Chakrabarty's work has become fundamental to discussion of the relationship between Western and non-Western history-writing. Earning his PhD from the

Australian National University, he had considerable significance for the writing of Australian indigenous history, including the 'History Wars.'

Subaltern Studies, which developed a strand of Said's thought, focused on the individual nature of the groups which had been written out of the 'standard' histories. Their choice of the term 'Subaltern', from the Italian Marxist Antonio Gramsci, reflects the populations outside the imposed hierarchy of industrial, capitalist power which was key to the operation of a colony. The Subaltern Studies Group was particularly interested in extracting evidence of the experience of ordinary Indians from the huge archive left behind by India's ruling classes and the British colonial administration. Gyan Prakash wrote that the historian 'had to conceive the subaltern differently and write different histories' of those people who had been excluded from administrative and cultural records.

Think laterally

1. What constitutes a 'historical' source is culturally relative. What problems might non-Western historians have with written sources?

_____

_____

_____

_____

History and individuals' memory

This growing recognition of the limitations of written sources (indeed, even in some cases, their absence) has encouraged historians to explore the usefulness of oral history. The practice of collecting, transcribing, and curating oral reports goes back to Herodotus and Thucydides, and arguably never ceased even in the west's most literate periods – perhaps *especially* in those periods, if one considers the popularity of the practice in the late eighteenth century in Germany. In modern times, however, a number of practitioners have been seminal in exploring the methods, theory, and implications of oral history.

The Belgian historian Jan Vansina (1929-2017) developed much of the method currently used by oral historians in his study of the peoples of Central Africa. His landmark text, *Oral Tradition as History*, was about the factual interpretation of oral history and showed the process by which historical evidence as understood by western historians could be found in oral artefacts. This process depended strongly on the historian's awareness of how narratives are reworked as they are retold, depending on the teller's perceived context, audience, and occasion.

Richard Price's book *Alabi's World* (1990) was a study of Surinam's Saramkha people, ethnic Yoruba from Africa who had been moved to the Dutch colony of Surinam in Latin America as slaves. Price wove together four voices: the oral accounts of the slaves' descendants, the Surinamese Saramaka, the colonial officials, and the German Moravian missionaries, in his history of this confluence of colonialism and different historical media and traditions. Price's unique method was to print the sources in different typefaces, which highlighted the different voices and encouraged readers to pay attention to the different ways in which they were constructed and could be compared.

2. How might such histories change the 'balance of power' perceived to belong to western academic history and those who practice it?

___

___

___

Increasing interest in oral history in the form of witness testimony has encouraged producers of 'popular' history to provide places where such testimony is comprehensively curated and displayed, such as museums, in tours of historic sites, historical theme parks, and now in online spaces. Perhaps because of its immediacy, emotional content, and personal subjectivity, *temoinage*, the literary genre of testimony by survivors of traumatic events, is often far more popular than the works of academic historians.

There are, however, significant problems with privileging of witness statements over other kinds of evidence, not the least of which is the unreliability of memory and the the context in which the statement is made. As one psychologist has noted, an eyewitness statement must be 'considered a joint product of cognitive factors and of interrogation.' In events such as the trials of war criminals, or government investigations into past atrocities like South Africa's 1995 Truth and Reconciliation Commission, developing a truthful narrative can be difficult for the historian or investigator who discovers that recollections have been unconsciously falsified. The weight of public sentiment is often in favour of the victims; the systemic inequality which created the situation in the first place continues to affect generations of people, and because confrontation may cause even greater trauma.

In the years since the parliamentary apology to members of the Stolen Generation of Australian Indigenous peoples, the continued inequality of care and life-chances for Indigenous peoples has added a contemporary political element to the writing of historical narratives about this time.

The Italian historian Alessandro Portelli has been one of the foremost practitioners of oral history in the twentieth century. His work 'has transformed oral history from being a kind of stepchild of history into a literary genre in its own right. He has allowed us to see oral histories as more than eyewitness accounts that are either true or false and to look for themes and structures of the stories.' Portelli's largely narratological approach to oral testimony strikes a socially acceptable and intellectually successful balance because he does not claim to be focused on its factual truth or falsity but to examine its ontological and formal character. In other words, Portelli is interested in what it means that the witness could speak of the event at all, and how they speak of something which *they believe* to be true:

> I was interested in narratives that were not factually true because it's one of the ways through which you can get at the meaning and the subjectivity as well as the facts of what actually happened.

The disparate interests of 'forgotten groups' have resulted in the questioning of grand narratives and sites of memory, especially in the oral transmission of historical experiences. This has had two consequences. First, it has raised questions, even doubts, about the possibility of historical truth; secondly, it has increased popular enthusiasm for the past, fuelled by new modes of communication, the interaction and interplay of which have created debates about the role of 'public' history.

Clarify

3. Consider the definition of 'truth' which you wrote earlier in this workbook. Do you still agree with it, in the light of your understanding about the cultural relativism of truth, and the possibility that historical truth may be unobtainable?

CONCEPT FOCUS 8: THE PUBLIC

Although universal literacy did not become a reality until the end of the nineteenth century, the public cannot really be said to have featured in the way history was conceptualized and written until the twentieth century. (Even now, universal literacy is still a largely political concept, since being able to read does not necessarily entail having the stamina, general knowledge, and conceptual understanding of causality and contingency that history requires). The public, therefore, was either the subject of history or a concept used in it, such as public life, as opposed to private life, or a popular public as opposed to academic elite. We can conceptualize the public and its relationship to how history is written in a number of ways:

The Public as the object or audience of written history. Since the advent of mass publishing, the public has been one of the arbiters of a historian's ability to make a living from telling the story of the past. Commercially-successful writers like Hume, Gibbon, Carlyle, and Macauley had a keen sense of the type and tenor of story that readers wanted to buy – a traveller in nineteenth-century Australia noted that on every squatter's shelf were the *Bible*, a condensation of Shakespeare's works, and Macauley's *Essays*. In the twentieth and twenty-first centuries, attracting the reading public to consume historical writing and viewing is now reckoned as an indicator of academic success, as universities once again prove themselves worth their funding by performing a social-outreach or service role.

The Public as respondents to history. Sometimes historical culture intended for public edification and consumption arouses their ire or discontent. One example was the 1993 Smithsonian exhibition of the *Enola Gay* B-29 bomber plane which dropped the atomic bomb on Hiroshima. Veterans groups were offended by the tenor of the Smithsonian's curation, which

> ...depicted the Japanese in a desperate defense of their home islands, saying little about what had made such a defense necessary. ... the US conduct of the war was depicted as brutal, vindictive, and racially motivated...

They were particularly incensed by the graphic displays of the Japanese dead and disfigured, and lobbied other interest groups including the American Legion, the Veterans of Foreign Wars, and the US Congress to condemn the display. Eventually, the Smithsonian scrapped the planned exhibition and replaced it with a more palatable narrative that confirmed the public memory of events. Because of the furore, the Enola Gay exhibit drew millions of visitors and remains the museum's most popular exhibit ever.

Read more about the relationship between history and public memory in this article:

https://www.asianstudies.org/publications/eaa/archives/history-and-memory-the-role-of-war-memorials-in-china-and-japan/

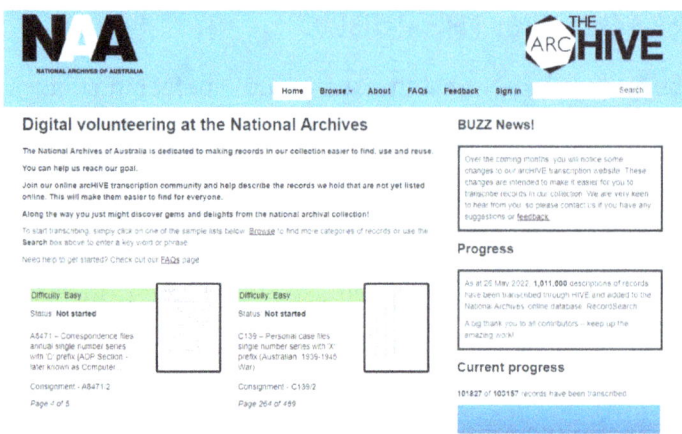

The Public as 'citizen historians'. With the advent of high-resolution reproduction of documents, it is now theoretically possible to build more complete archives of imaged, transcribed, and translated historical sources than ever before. However, the amount of human hours this requires far outstrips even the most generous funding, and ordinary citizens are often encouraged to collaborate on projects which had once been the preserve of gentlemen's clubs and societies, or specialist academics. The National Archives of Australia, like most national archives, has a dedicated page for digital volunteers, called the arcHIVE, in which people can log in and transcribe a simple document.

The Public as history-makers. As well as being the object of historians' interest, the public can also act as their own historians, simultaneously historicising their lived experience of a specific time, event, or identity. The 2020 COVID pandemic produced many large-scale projects by public institutions – and keen amateurs – where people archived evidence of their experience of what was perceived to be a generation-defining event.

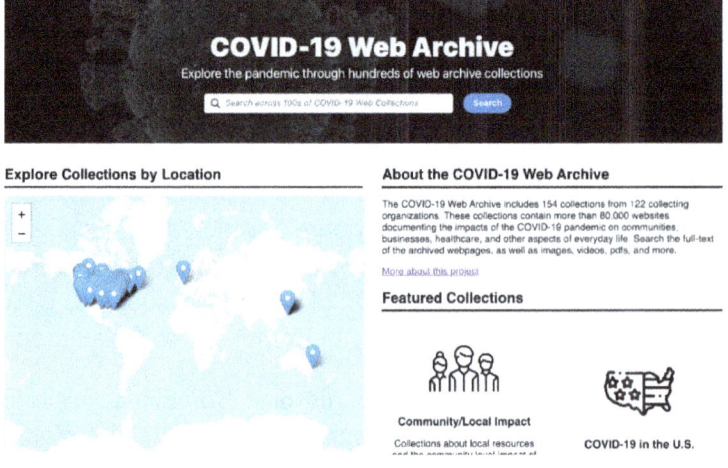

The website **https://covid-19archive.org** was instituted by a group of American academics, and invited readers of 'Journal of the Plague Year to become your personal diary--a place where you share moments of your life, along with hundreds of others to create a historical record of the pandemic.' Peter Hobbins, a medical historian, started the **#covidstreetarchive** in which people could contribute photographs of their streets and neighbourhoods closed and under lockdown. State and national libraries and archives also ran pandemic projects such as the State Library of Victoria's *Memory Bank: The Collective Isolation Project* and Historic Canada's *Canada During Covid Archive*. Of interest is the number of archives in anglophone, developed nations which value the concept of individual experience and expression, again reflecting the difference in perceptions of both the public, narrative, and history.

National and collective memory

The memory of individuals, however, is shaped symbiotically with the collective memory, which has been an object of study since the 1920s. In 1925 the French sociologist Maurice Halbwachs (*left*) suggested that a collective social memory alters over time. It therefore has a history of its own and acts as a historical force in its own right. Halbwachs, who studied philosophy with Henri Bergson (whose distinction between subjective time and 'clock time' or objective time had a significant impact on modern understanding of memory), was originally a sociologist and in his posthumously-published book *La mémoire collective* he advanced two laws governing the form and evolution of collective memory: the Law of Fragmentation, and the Law of Concentration. These have been developed in studies throughout the twentieth and twenty-first centuries into a set of habits or behaviours which occur whenever groups collaborate to recall information, particularly information concerned with the group's identity. Halbwachs died at Buchenwald concentration camp during WWII.

Fifty years later Paul Fussell revisited Halbwach's idea in *The Great War and Modern Memory* (1975), a pioneering study of how literature, especially war poetry, produced in Britain during World War I became the evidence that subsequent generations used to 'remember' collectively the First World War. By extension, it shows how such partial and partisan 'memories' have shaped forms of political and social cognition in the present. Now that the surviving participants of World War I have died, the archive of 'primary' sources is complete and historians are gradually turning to second-order study of the event and the ways in which it has become history. The historians Jay Winter and, more recently David Reynolds, have developed the Halbwachs/Fussell thesis in very sophisticated ways.

Pierre Nora's seven-volume *Les lieux de mémoire* [Sites of Memory] (1984-1992) is a study of the cultural objects used by the French collective memory to shape and articulate their sense of cultural identity. Nora's choice of objects ranged from physical objects such as the Palace of Versailles or the Eiffel Tower, to rituals such as Bastille Day or the Tour de France and even a textbook, *La Tour de la France par deux enfants* (1901).

Comprising nearly two hundred articles, *Les Lieux de Mémoire* suggests that the change associated with modernity destroyed connections between French society and its 'living sense of collective memory'. Nora responded to criticisms that *Les Lieux de mémoire* was an attempt to create a national history of the type, long rejected by the *Annales* school, that ignored issues of gender and French overseas imperialism, calling it instead a 'democratisation of history':

> National memory cannot come into being until the historical framework of the nation has been shattered. It reflects the abandonment of the traditional channels and modes of transmission of the past and the desacralisation of such primary sites of initiation as the school, the family, the museum, and the monument: what was once the responsibility of these institutions has now flowed over into the public domain and been taken over by the media and tourist industry.

History and the Culture Wars

In addition to the challenges and opportunities already outlined, the late twentieth and twenty-first centuries have also witnessed the emergence of approaches that challenge accepted narratives about the past – approaches which have influenced *what* is studied rather than the *how* and the *why*. The ever-increasing new perspectives germinating in the Academy have resulted in the 'culture wars.'

Inaugurated by the election of Margaret Thatcher in 1979 and of Ronald Reagan in 1980, the culture wars, reflected the new dominance of conservative thinking and political power. Thatcher, whose turn of phrase was legendary (including her statement 'The facts of life are conservative') was previously education minister in Edward Heath's government. A chemist by training, she was intrinsically suspicious of the postmodern 'turn', and, like other Conservatives, disagreed with the challenge to acknowledge minority perspectives and modes of expressing them, or to consider the uses of different types of source from different provenances. She said:

> although not an historian myself, I had a very clear – and I had naïvely imagined uncontroversial – idea of what history was. History is an account of what happened in the past ... [It involved] memorising what actually happened.

The implicit danger of the Reagan-Thatcher conservative turn, however, was revealed by the West German scholar Ernst Nolte's claim that the attempt to eradicate an entire people was not unique to Nazi Germany, but rather that Hitler was imitating the Soviet Union. In 1985 West German Chancellor Helmut Kohl and US President Ronald Reagan (who had said 'The Nazis were victims too') visited the Bitburg Cemetery, where members of the SS and other German soldiers were buried. Kohl may have been attempting to reverse the politics of his predecessor, and Reagan's diaries, published in 2007, reflect his belief in the moral uprightness of his visit. It was an indication of how deeply conservative (and later neo-conservative) politicians felt about their cause, despite their portrayal as cynical purveyors of the 'Great Lie' by recent historians and commentators.

Opposition towards Nolte and the conservatives, particularly by the philosopher Jürgen Habermas, resulted in the *historikerstreit* (Battle of the Historians) which drew public attention until superseded by the more immediate issues of German reunification after 1989. It is perhaps important to note that almost all the historians involved exploited the media opportunities to prolong the debate and invoke the participation of all areas of society. A public exhibition in 1995 produced documentation of the Wehrmacht's involvement in the Holocaust, conclusively dispensing with the idea that the SS alone were responsible.

Germany's *historikerstreit* has had its equivalent in the Anglophone world's 'History Wars.' In Australia this has focused on historians' treatment of the Aboriginal population by British colonists after 1788, most notably in the ABC-televised debate between Henry Reynolds, author of *Why Weren't We Told?*, and his major critic Keith Windschuttle in his three-volume *The Fabrication of Aboriginal History*. France and Israel have witnessed equivalent debates, where public demands for a historical narrative featuring heroes and villains clashed with the stridently conservative attack in the culture wars. This debate gained greater currency when the Soviet-dominated system of satellite states in Eastern Europe collapsed after 1989. The disintegration of the Soviet Union itself in 1991 seemed further to discredit any challenge to Western liberal-democratic-capitalism.

Oriel College's statue of Cecil Rhodes, which in 2021 provoked a strike by lecturers and student action from those calling for its removal. As of 2023, the statue is still there.

In the digital age, the culture war has taken the form of stringent and often acrimonious policing of what can be said, by whom, and about whom. Even those who disagree that we are experiencing a culture war, or that it is largely a dispute between two sides of an educated elite, are aware of the problems of 'political correctness' which governs what can be expressed by members of social and cultural categories. One commentator has noted that

> There have always been cultural conflicts but it's become much sharper in the last 20 years thanks to declining trust in institutions that were meant to hold together the cohesion of society, some of the growing inequalities, and most of all the proliferation of technology that enables and indeed encourages people to cluster in their cultural groups.

The historian Dominic Sandbrook has pointed out that there have always been culture wars, and cites the Roman empire's transition from paganism to Christianity which involved clashes over statues and shrines. There are, he argues, 'moments in history when disputes about history, identity, symbols, images and so on loom very large. Think about so much of 17th-century politics, for example, when people would die over the wording of a prayer book.' The process of circling back to old debates, at a new and more ferocious speed, is often missed by the participants in the digital battlefield; Tom Holland has noted the irony that 'woke social justice warriors don't realize that they're really 16th- and 17th-century Christian Puritans.'

4. What is your experience of having speech policed in online or public places? How has it changed the way you think about the past?

___

___

___

Extend yourself

5. *While some stories are told... others are silenced. The question of why this is the case (the emphases and repetitions as well as the silences) has been and is a preoccupation of my generation of historians.* Giselle Byrnes.

How is this the case with historians involved in the culture wars?

Popular History

Part of the postmodern effect of 'cultural flattening' – the collapse of the socio-intellectual distinction between 'high' and 'low' culture – is evident in historical writing and historical 'culture'. 'Historical culture' is a mostly non-textual process by which the historical aspect of a thing (from a single object to an entire town) is turned into an object through re-enactment, recreation, curation and display, or other means that allow the general public to participate in its historicizing. The key aspects of popular history are its inclusiveness and non-academic, sometimes even anti-academic, character (*Horrible Histories* for children, and such documentaries as *Grossest Jobs in History*, are examples).

There have been many criticisms of popular history, which has been described as 'porridgey pabulum for the lowest common denominator' and 'self-satisfied nostalgia-fests lacking academic rigour' which, in the twenty-first century tends to be 'Whiggishly deferential to the subject and patronising to the reader.' Alastair Harper, a writer for the *Guardian*, described the difference between popular history and the academic:

> Academic history is perceived to have become myopically focused on minutiae, drowning in clunky jargon, dissertations and careers being based on the most unappealingly desiccated and obscure fragments of the world's past. The academic grove no longer warmly welcomes the rest of the world – so it has became the role of the amateur, the red-blooded lover of history as it happened – to fill it.

There has always been an eager and intelligent readership for written history, as Shakespeare's extensive use of Raphael Holinshed's chronicle shows. Since the 1960s social changes have created a genre of historical activity which we now loosely call 'popular'. Among these changes are: the advent of television and its usurpation of the printed word as the main means of mass entertainment and information; the acknowledgement of history's disciplinary responsibility to society; cultural pluralism; the technological capacity to recreate historical artefacts and environments on a scale never before achieved, and the commercial reward for doing so, and the distinction between 'general' and 'academic' lists by publishers, rather than the strict separation of the two into different publishing worlds.

Because popular history aims to reach a wide, rather than specialized, audience, the need for a 'face' or personality to tell the story is often the most important element. The slightly nebulous 'communication skills' which arose as an in-demand talent in the late twentieth century took over from insightful analysis, expertise in document-handling, archaeology, or even period history, as necessary for popular historians.

Academic historians' capacity to 'translate' their area of interest in terms that the average person can understand is increasingly important to the security of academic jobs, as universities try to diversify their sources of income and off-set the possibility of a future crash in the humanities. While this seems pessimistic, it is only a small part of the rationale for using academic historians to present popular history; many have been talented and personable presenters who have made significant contributions to the wider culture. A.J.P. Taylor was an early pioneer of history on radio television: in 1942 Taylor made the first of seven appearances on *The World at War – Your Questions Answered* broadcast by BBC Forces' Radio. After the war he became one of the first BBC television historians, as a panellist on *In The News* (1950-1954). Eric Hobsbawm and E.P. Thompson were also presenters and today, Simon Schama, Niall Ferguson, and Mary Beard have all presented multiple television history documentaries while holding prestigious academic posts. However, many successful (in commercial terms, which is how this genre of history tends to be evaluated) popular historians have never held academic posts: John Julius Norwich, Michael Wood, David McCullough, and Barbara W. Tuchman have never held academic posts and are highly-regarded broadcasters, writers, and project patrons of inclusive, popular, public history. More recently, the comic character of Philomena Cunk has parodied these telly-dons, showing that they are now an accepted and even conventional institution with recognizable delivery and approach.

Think laterally

6. What is your opinion of historians like Simon Schama, who respond to a charge of subjectivity by saying that their 'telly-history' is personal? Can such a personal history be representative, and therefore of interest, to anyone else? Should we privilege the historian as a person simply because they are a professional historian?

Film and History

Nowhere, however, is a public vs academic divide more pronounced than in History vs. Hollywood. In 1935 Louis R. Gottschalk, an American academic historian, complained to the president of MGM about historical accuracy in its productions, saying that 'no picture of an historical nature [should be] to be offered to the public until a reputable historian has had a chance to criticise and revise it.' History does not seem to have recorded the MGM president's response.

Yet Robert Rosenstone, who has written extensively on the History vs. Hollywood debate, has pointed out that absolute factual accuracy is an unrealistic criterion by which to rate films about history. The simple need 'to fill out the specifics of a particular historical scene' will always demand some invention, simply because we cannot know how *everything* was in the past – particularly in specific past events. Nor is it necessarily important, or at least, not to all historians. Some historians will argue about inaccuracies of dress while maintaining that the invention of minor characters or collapsing two characters into one are permitted; others will say that accurate reflection of time and place is more important to convey than what people wore.

In his essay 'The Historical Film as Real History', Rosenstone argued not only that historical film is, on the whole, far more valuable to the cause of historical awareness than it is dangerous, but that

> Film is out of the control of historians. Film shows that academics do not own the past. Film creates a historical world with which the written word cannot compete, at least for popularity. Film is a disturbing symbol of an increasingly postliterate world (in which people can read but won't).

Drawing on the work of Hayden White, who discussed 'the representation of history and our thought about it in visual images and filmic discourse' which he called *historiophoty*, Rosenstone has argued that

> It is time to create a new frame, one which includes the larger realm of past and present in which both sorts of history are located and to which both refer. Seen this way, the question cannot be, Does the historical film convey facts or make arguments as well as written history? Rather, the

appropriate questions are: What sort of historical world does each film construct and how does it construct that world? How can we make judgments about that construction? How and what does that historical construction mean to us? After these three questions are answered, we may wish to ask a fourth: How does the historical world on the screen relate to written history?

Certainly, as film becomes more and more a part of 'representing' history in the classroom and popular culture, as well as recording it in a digital world, the questions Rosenstone asks will become ever-more insistent in mainstream historical discourse.

Part of the skepticism with which professional historians react to 'telly-history' and 'Hollywood-history' derives from a backlog of factually questionable but hugely popular 'awareness raising' productions. Two television miniseries produced during the 1970s - Alex Haley's *Roots* (which has recently been remade) and Gerald Green's fictionalised *Holocaust* – stimulated ordinary people to find out about their own pasts, particularly in those groups which had been denied a history or serious historical attention, and also provoked debates about international events which politics had caused the academy to ignore. Yet there were serious factual flaws in both, and many critics argued that the neat dramatization of the story overlooked the messy and frequently ambiguous reality of events. For the sake of presenting a story 'emplotted' in a way that popular audiences could respond to, with clearly-drawn heroes and a conventional storyline, the tragedies of enslavement and genocide were at risk of being trivialized.

Think laterally

7. Look up 'Sorites paradox' in Wikipedia. How does this paradox apply to historical film?

___

___

___

___

___

___

For every historian who criticizes the popularisation of history, there are just as many who validate it, comment on its methods, and work with commercial producers of 'material history' to present the work to the public with integrity and accuracy. Natalie Zemon Davis, whose book *The Return of Martin Guerre* was turned into a popular film with Gerard Depardieu, acted as a consultant to the film producers. In her essay 'Stories and the Hunger to Know', she has argued that *both* historians' interpretation *and* the quest for evidence should be present and acknowledged in order to prevent people from believing that either one has a monopoly on the truth. Feature films, she has said, are good 'thought experiments' as long as they are connected with the general historical evidence.

In his book *The Past Is a Foreign Country* (1985), David Lowenthal, who was credited with developing the discipline of heritage studies, responded to the denigration of popular history by arguing that 'We must concede the ancients their place ... but their past is not simply back there, in a separate and foreign country, it is assimilated in ourselves and resurrected in an ever-changing present.' He pointed out that when we put signs in museums to 'explain' what are now 'exhibits' rather than objects *in situ* and in use, we impose a meaning upon them which seems appropriate to the imagined or anticipated present-day audience.

While sharing some characteristics with film, such as a generally chronological narrative, the documentary or even docudrama format is significantly different because any dramatic license such as acting or reconstructions is usually subordinated to the awareness of the non-fictional frame. As the historian and sociologist of film Pierre Sorlin has commented, the documentary medium allows greater engagement with visual sources: they are presented *as* sources, and usually the viewer is allowed more time to view them thoughtfully than in a feature film, where they are secondary to the characters.

Other historians and media executives with a background or in history have identified in the technologies of film and television great opportunities to bring serious history to a mass audience. Examples include the Australian Frank Hurley's feature documentary film *South* (1919) which brought the dramatic story of the failed Shackleton expedition to the Antarctic to millions of viewers. Hurley made several documentary films about Australian troops serving in WWI; his legacy as a film-maker and documentarian has caused some controversy in the last decade, with the realization that much of his 'documentary footage' was restaged (several actions by ANZAC forces in Egypt and Palestine were restaged at Bondi Beach), and some of his still images were composite. The recent documentary *Frank Hurley: The Man Who Made History* by Simon Nasht presents both sides of the argument and reflects the different views taken by Australian and British historians and archivists.

The development of Cinéma Vérité in the 1950s made documentaries more exciting but the presence of editors who transform the footage into a film meant that there is a significant degree of editorial input: viewers must be made aware that the director has chosen how much involvement to have with their subject. Fundamentals of the style include following a person during a crisis with a moving, often handheld, camera to capture more personal reactions. There are no sit-down interviews, and the shooting ratio (the amount of film shot to the finished product) is very high, often reaching 80:1.

Claude Lanzmann's *Shoah* (1986) included interviews not only with surviving Jewish victims but also German perpetrators and even bystanders such as Polish peasants, witnesses to Jews being taken to the deaths, which was not only more powerful than a miniseries, but more political because it provided evidence than many people involved in atrocities were alive and not remotely contrite about their participation. Ken Burns' extraordinarily popular

Civil War (1990) was the first of his distinguished career of historical and biographical documentaries. Burns uses popular historians, including David McCullough and Shelby Foote to break 'the stranglehold of the academician exercised over this discipline for the last hundred years.' Although one academic was displeased with 'high velocity words like agony and horror and gargantuan and fantastic and colossal,' Burns has made many more people aware of historical narratives and issues than his language has deterred.

The transatlantic historian and media personality Simon Schama, who has held positions at Harvard and Colombia, has used aspects of his own life and background in his television documentary series. Where he has acknowledged that his presentation is of a personal nature, and does not seek to simplify complex issues but rather show them through his own perspective, his work has generally been accepted for what it is. Some of his more literary experiments, such as 1991 *Dead Certainties (Unwarranted Speculations)* have been less favourably received – here he introduced invented dialogue and events in a reconstructed past, thus transgressing too much into fiction, many historians argued. Schama's work has shown how television can create creating public interest in the past. His essay *Clio at the Multiplex* is clear evidence of his awareness that film can greatly extend the scope of traditional, academic history.

Schama and similar 'telly-dons' have made themselves cultural and economic human commodities, famous for their personality and character as much as for their profession. Historiographers have responded by questioning whether marketing considerations have begun to supersede other issues in the presentation of the past. But it has also encouraged speculation of a major paradigm shift in consciousness about how we think about the past. Bettany Hughes has contributed two pieces to the developing debate: the 2011 Royal Television Society Huw Wheldon Memorial Lecture entitled 'TV: modern father of history?', and the 2012 Medlicott Address.

Clarify

8. Comment on the idea that historians are now caught in their own trap of having created a culture which reveres professional authority, but which rarely understands the writing it produces.

ISBN 9780645591422

Reading task 8

Read the following passage, from Chakrabarty's *Provincializing Europe*.

The Indian constitution tellingly begins by repeating certain universal Enlightenment themes celebrated, say, in the American constitution. And it is salutary to remember that the writings of the most trenchant critic of the institution of "untouchability" in British India refer us back to some originally European ideas about liberty and human equality. I too write from within this inheritance. Postcolonial scholarship is committed, almost by definition, to engaging the universals—such as the abstract figure of the human or that of Reason—that were forged in eighteenth-century Europe and that underlie the human sciences. ...Fanon's struggle to hold on to the Enlightenment idea of the human—even when he knew that European imperialism had reduced that idea to the figure of the settler-colonial white man—is now itself a part of the global heritage of all postcolonial thinkers. The struggle ensues because there is no easy way of dispensing with these universals in the condition of political modernity. Without them there would be no social science that addresses issues of modern social justice.

I am aware that an entity called "the European intellectual tradition" stretching back to the ancient Greeks is a fabrication of relatively recent European history. ... few if any Indian social scientists or social scientists of India would argue seriously with, say, the thirteenth-century logician Gangesa or with the grammarian and linguistic philosopher Bartrihari (fifth to sixth centuries), or with the tenth- or eleventh-century aesthetician Abhinavagupta. ...They treat these traditions as truly dead, as history. ...And yet past European thinkers and their categories are never quite dead for us in the same way. South Asian(ist) social scientists would argue passionately with a Marx or a Weber without feeling any need to historicize them or to place them in their European intellectual contexts.

1. Briefly identify the challenges which the colonial legacy has left for South-Asian historians and anthropologists.

2. In your own words, explain the basis of Chakrabarty's feeling that a social injustice was perpetrated upon South-Asian people.

3. In what ways might South-Asian theorists and thinkers like those mentioned (Gangesa, Bhartrihari et al) have been denied the same stature as Marx and Weber?

4. Look at the website of the Institute of Historical Research, part of the University of London, at https://www.history.ac.uk/ Find two things on the website which bear out Chakrabarty's claims, and two which dispute them. Explain your choices.

NOTES

Chapter revision statement

Write a list of the key points from this chapter.

_____
_____
_____
_____
_____
_____
_____
_____
_____

Use the list to write a short statement about important features in the discipline of History during the period studied in this chapter.

_____
_____
_____
_____
_____
_____
_____

Notes

_____
_____
_____
_____
_____
_____
_____

Chapter 9: Recent times 2 – what will be left?

Micro-History

Micro-history's small focus is intended to show the *multum in parvo* – how the wider context of politics, society, 'mentalities', economics, religion, and material culture informed the experience of an individual, group, or event. Although the term was coined in the 1970s in Italy, and many of the method's earliest proponents were Italian, the approach is reminiscent of the 'social novel' of the late nineteenth century, in which a single character or problem reflects trends in the contextualizing society.

Carlo Ginzburg's *The Cheese and the Worms* (1976) is perhaps the most popular work of microhistory and focuses on the life of a sixteenth-century miller who is tried for heresy. By focusing on the individual and the single event, Ginzburg drew out a history of the semi-rural Italian society of the time, the conflict between different philosophical views of the world and how these views spread through printing technology, and the perception of the injustice of heresy trials. Because of their focus on individuals – who quickly become 'protagonists' in the literary sense – microhistory attracts adaptations to film and novel (such as Christopher Nolan's *Dunkirk* and *The Return of Martine Guerre*), and is interesting to readers of both academic and non-specialist backgrounds, and the scope makes it appealing to the exercise of the graduate thesis, which perhaps accounts for its continuing popularity.

The Italian *microstorie* was taken up by German historians in the 1980s, becoming *Alltagsgeschichte*, which focused on the experiences of those without privilege – history told 'from below'. This use of microhistory to show imbalances of social privilege, to show the lived experience of marginalised groups, and to correct inaccurate narratives was also applied to ecological problems. William Cronon's *Changes in the Land: Indian, colonists and the Ecology of New England* (1983), revealed that 'ecological abundance and economic prodigality went hand-in-hand: the people of plenty were people of waste.' He proposed that the way cultures conceptualize property and ownership is a major factor in economies and ecosystems. Unlike most historians, he documented how Native Americans actively intervened in and shaped the ecosystems in which they lived, challenging the simplistic countercultural narrative of indigenous people who did not 'interfere' with their environment.

Think laterally

1. Find out about the German term *Schlüsselwörter* or 'key-words', words which can act as the key to an entire philosophical matrix.

Historians formulate a problem that seems interesting - a hypothesis, if you will - and then they look for evidence. The historical evidence will not always fit the original hypothesis, and thus the historian modifies the hypothesis. The result is a process of dialectical feedback in which evidence and hypothesis constantly modify each other. Historians tend to discard evidence that seems irrelevant to their purposes even though other historians might consider that evidence to be of vital importance. Other evidence may force the historian to revise an argument. In the end, historians never seem to write the book they set out to write.

Norman Wilson

2. How does micro-history attempt to get around this problem? How is it a response to previous types of history-writing?

History at the Turn of the Third Millennium

If we imagine a scale which runs from microhistory's focus on individuals at one end, to impersonal abstractions about 'history' and 'mankind' on the other, the beginning of the twenty-first century showed a new attempt to address – and even end – the problem of 'historical man'. Francis Fukuyama's *The End of History and the Last Man* (1992) claimed that the end of the Cold War had shown the superiority of liberal democracy and capitalism. To Fukuyama the collapse of the Eastern Bloc signalled an 'end of history.' There might still be changes in international relations, but if the superiority of liberal democratic capitalism was accepted by everyone, there would no longer be major conflicts over values. If History even lasted in the academy, Fukuyama said, it would be in purely narrative form, demonstrating the superiority of the 'now' compared to 'the bad old days'. Fukuyama has since conceded that he was radically premature in his projections – which he might have realized had he read Mary Shelley's apocalyptic, dystopian novel *The Last Man* (1826).

A more sober response to the radical disjunction between postmodernism and positivism is reflected in Joyce Appleby, Lynn Hunt and Margaret Jacob's *Telling the Truth about History* (1994). Appleby et al proposed a middle position between postmodernists' claim that historical truth was impossible to know and the positivists' claim that the 'facts of the past' speak for themselves. Their 'practical realism' or 'qualified objectivity' said that: an absolutely objective conclusion will always be beyond the historian, but this does not mean that any chain of reasoning is equally valid. No story is just 'as good as any other.' The presence and provenance of evidence place constraints on historians and, properly acknowledged, those constraints must be factored into the interpretation, which produces a narrative.

Three years later, Richard Evans' *In Defence of History* (1997) argued that, in fact, history could indeed produce true conclusions.

> [H]istory is an empirical discipline, and it is concerned with the content of knowledge rather than its nature ... Objective history is, in the last analysis, history that is researched and written within the limits placed on historical imagination by the facts of history and the sources which reveal them, and by the historian's desire to produce a true, fair, and adequate account of the subject under consideration.

Although the logic of this is spurious – such terms as 'objective, 'facts', and 'true, fair, and adequate' beg the very question Evans seeks to answer – it is historiographically important that Evans made this strong statement after Appleby et al. The emergence of such works effectively indicated that debate between the literary, cultural, post-modernists and the discipline of history had concluded, which may be seen in Keith Jenkins' suggestion that we should:

> ... simply 'wave goodbye to history', contending 'there is no reason why...
> post-modernism needs to drag modernity's very particular and peculiar
> habits of historicizing time with it.

However, notwithstanding Jenkins' virtual concession of defeat in the History Wars in 1998, the third millennium opened with a reminder of just how seriously the later twentieth century had challenged history and how it is practised.

Clarify

3. For your own understanding, outline the opposing arguments of Appleby/Evans and Jenkins.

Think laterally

4. Outline the difference between a true, a valid, and a sound argument.

Professional Standards and Professional Disputes

During the 1960s and 1970s the British writer David Irving cultivated an association with European neo-fascist groups, using a positivist approach to history to cast doubt on the fact or extent of the Holocaust and Hitler's involvement in it. During the late 1980s and 1990s Irving seized on the assertions of postmodernists about the impossibility of achieving absolute truth, and allied these theoretical claims with practical doubts about the reliability of victims' oral testimony. In his subsequent apparent denial of the Holocaust, first mooted in a footnote in his *Hitler's War* (1977), Irving courted both the ire of Holocaust historians and the law. Deborah Lipstadt's *Denying the Holocaust: The Growing Assault on Truth and Memory* (1993) argued that radical postmodernist revision made it 'difficult to talk about the objective truth of a text, legal concept, or even an event.' This radical scepticism, she said, gave Holocaust deniers like Irving a means to distort the past.

Irving brought a libel lawsuit against Lippstadt (*above*) and her publisher, Penguin Books. Given the English legal system's principle that in libel the onus of proof rests with the defence, Lipstadt and Penguin Books assembled a defence team of leading historians, including Richard Evans and the Dutch architectural historian Robert Jan van Pelt. In presenting the defence, Evans and his fellow historians explained to the High Court the scholarship of interpreting historical evidence in order to demonstrate both the truth of the claims Irving disputed and Irving's long-standing association with neo-Nazi groups.

In its unequivocal judgement in favour of the defendants, the High Court gave legal basis to the proposition that the procedures of historical scholarship can indeed establish dependable knowledge about the past. The verdict in the Irving trial reassured historians that postmodernism had not completely undermined the discipline's ability to establish truth about the past, so long as strict adherence to rules of procedure are followed.

Recent years have witnessed several other widely-publicised scandals involving well-regarded historians who violated the discipline's rules and good scholarly practice. Michael Bellesiles' *Arming America: The Origins of a National Gun Culture* (2002) argued that most

Americans did not possess firearms until after the Civil War. This interpretation entangled him in the shrill and bitter argument over Second Amendment rights. Several scholars pointed out significant errors in facts and sources, and a 2002 panel concluded that Bellesiles was 'guilty of unprofessional and misleading work', raising questions about falsified data. Columbia University withdrew its award of the Bancroft History Prize and Bellesiles resigned from Emory University.

In 2002 *The Weekly Standard* and the *Los Angeles Times* determined that Doris Kearns Goodwin's *The Fitzgeralds and the Kennedys* used, without attribution, numerous phrases and sentences from three other books. Lynne McTaggart remarked, 'If somebody takes a third of somebody's book, which is what happened to me, they are lifting out the heart and guts of somebody else's individual expression.' Having reached a private settlement with McTaggart over the issue, Goodwin then wrote in *Time* magazine that '[t]hough my footnotes repeatedly cited Ms. McTaggart's work, I failed to provide quotation marks for phrases that I had taken verbatim ... The larger question for those of us who write history is to understand how citation mistakes can happen.' In its analysis of the controversy, *Slate* magazine criticized Goodwin for the aggrieved tone of her explanation, and suggested Goodwin's worst offence was allowing the plagiarism to remain in future editions of the book even after it was brought to her attention. *Slate* further reported that multiple passages in Goodwin's *No Ordinary Time*, about the Roosevelt family, were also taken from other books, although Goodwin 'scrupulously' footnoted the material.

Clarify

5. What would you say are History's vital 'rules of procedure'? How have the people mentioned in this section flouted or followed them?

History in the Digital Age

Many of these thefts, 'borrowings', collective lazinesses and errors can be attributed in part to the digital environment in which History is now researched and written. Although the world of electronic text production and reproduction has made it easier to find evidence, some critics believe that it has diminished the scholarly standard of the text produced.

Since 1993 historians have been able to upload documentary sources and make them freely available to those with an internet connection – or, in increasing cases, the economic means to by-pass the paywall. Certainly, there are limitations: those who do not know about particular groups in the scholarly community are ignorant of the information; those who cannot negotiate the technology are excluded from access, and those who cannot decode the technological discourse are at a disadvantage compared to those who are fluent in writing and reading digital texts. Those who are unaware of the physical and digital architecture of large-scale databases are cut off from their sources and evidence in a way that historians before the digital age were not.

National records and archives are now less physical repositories of actual documents and more geolocations where databases of those documents are hosted. The National Records of Scotland hosts a digital record of over fifty different archives, many of which are off-site and in private hands.

One example of how digital databases make unseen connections for historians can be seen in the website of the National Records of Scotland: (https://www.nrscotland.gov.uk/). This collection of records and muniments is held by the National Library of Scotland. The library was formed from the Advocates Library in Edinburgh, since lawyers tended to be the custodians of personal and family papers, and were often personally interested in antiquarian records. Many records, however, are still in the physical possession of the families, antiquarian clubs, and trusts which created them. Along with these personal papers are the government-created records of births, deaths, and marriages which are normally created in the first instance in a registry office.

Although there is a geolocation for the institution which hosts the databases, many of the physical records are widely dispersed. Before the digital age, some of these records were difficult to access, interpret, and even comprehend, but the online databases allow researchers around the world to check and find most of the records, whether in summary or full-text form. What was once the highly specialized preserve of archivists, with knowledge largely stored in individuals' memories and so potentially lost with them, is now collated and interpreted by databases. However, it can also give a false idea of equality between records and coherence of the whole corpus. The ease and plenitude of access to digital records also encourages researchers to disregard the few remaining records which have not been digitised. As Ian Milligan notes in *The Transformation of Historical Research in the Digital Age,*

> It might not seem like a significant decision to explore the *Toronto Star* rather than the *Toronto Telegraph*, but if every historian makes the same decision, this represents a dramatic shift. These thousands of individual decisions mean that over time scholarship begins to homogenize in terms of what we cite. ... While many of these shifts build on pre-digital trends, historical information is always mediated, whether this is due to the choice of what to microfilm or to broader archival biases – yet the transformation of the digital age represents a dramatic acceleration.

These immense innovations have created new possibilities certainly, but also potential problems. Daniel Cohen and Roy Rosenzweig's *Digital History: A Guide to Gathering, Preserving and Presenting the Past on the Web* lists the advantages of the web as 'Access... flexibility, diversity, manipulabilty, interactivity and hyper-textuality (or non-linearity).' But open access and unchecked participation in the production and revision of historical work can undermine the integrity of the checks and balances which the discipline developed precisely to combat these potential 'slippages'. It has also changed how historians 'parse information', to use Ian Milligan's phrase. The historian who has read all (or most) of a text to find a reference has a difference understanding of context than the historian who has found the same information by means of a keyword search. In 1996 Gertrude Himmelfarb, a critic of radical change, warned

> the Internet does not distinguish between the true and false, the important and the trivial, the enduring and the ephemeral... Every source appearing on the screen has the same weight and credibility as every other; no authority is 'privileged' over any other.

While Himmelfarb's warning perhaps smacks of an attempt to maintain a privileged position and authority, the internet academic community (once an oxymoronic term) has striven to respond to these warnings. Yet the digital manner of document collections' presentation is not only new to history-writing, but also different from the way in which those documents related to each other in their original contexts.

The recent appearance of very sophisticated chatbots, which can produce texts that rival those of (good) academic writers for clarity, coherence, and the semblance of authority is an important new element in the profession. Highly fluent bots can mimic the linguistic tone and tenor of historical figures from Jesus of Nazareth to Charles Darwin, drawing on a database of the original figure's verbal legacy to give authoritative-sounding answers to questions put by the curious and sometimes desperate. Since A.I. by nature poses problems about what we perceive to be 'real' in terms of intelligence and interaction, it is reasonable to say that the texts A.I. produces are equally problematic in terms of truth and authenticity.

Certainly, this is no more than many religious and philosophical practitioners have done – extracting appropriate evidence from a corpus like the Bible or the Platonic dialogues to answer questions. But the problem of veracity and authority, however, becomes significantly greater when A.I. extrapolates or infers answers from the existing verbal corpus, and produces answers to questions which the historical figure simply did not encounter. Hellohistory.ai, for example, claims that 'You can ask questions, have discussions, or even debate with historical figures about different topics, gaining new insights and perspectives on history and life. Our AI technology ensures that each conversation is tailored to your interests, making it an immersive and educational experience.' A chatbot recently delivered a sermon during a religious service in Germany, and A.I. Jesus has attracted viewers on Twitch and dealt with whether gay people can enter Heaven – it seems a matter of time before Artificial Herodotus is quoted as authoritatively as the 'real' historian.

Think laterally

6. Suggest some implications of finding and using sources which have been so drastically removed from their original, non-digital, context. What effect might it have on the resulting narrative?

Think laterally

7. Choose ONE historian from before the 20th century. What would their reaction be to a digital archive?

Extend yourself

To write at length about an area of changing historical interpretation, you will have to do some minor research. How much of this research will be performed digitally? How does that change your perception of the debate? How much of the context will you actually read – or will you only read paragraphs around the keywords? As you skip around different databases and texts, consider this remark by the literary critic George Landow:

> Hypertext emphasizes that the marginal has as much to offer as the central by refusing to grant centrality to anything for more than the time a gaze rests upon it. In hypertext, centrality, like beauty and relevance, resides in the eye of the beholder. ... conceptual systems "founded upon ideas of center, margin, hierarchy, and linearity" [are changed to] "ones of multilinearity, nodes, links, and networks."

8. What does this mean? Paraphrase Landow's description in terms that apply to historians.

ISBN 9780645591422

CONTENT FOCUS 9: TIME

Although the relationship between time and the discipline of history may seem like a simple one – history is the study of the past through the documentation left over from that past – the way time is perceived, grouped, named, and measured is complex. Almost every historian has had a unique understanding of time, which has in turn been shaped by his context. Thus the writing that historians do in their present is influenced by their personal perception of the past, which perceived past is the product of the historian's own personal past!

The four ways of perceiving the time are often described as: linear; cyclic; progressive, and degenerative. Yet the actual spans of time which fall within each aspect can vary widely. For each aspect, suggest at least one historian who has used this as their chief understanding of time.

Linear time could apply to a single individual's lifespan, or to the duration of a dynasty's prominence. In classical Hebrew, linear time is regarded as the medium in which predestined events take place. (This introduces a second idea, of narrative time or a period during which a narrative takes place – such narratives are often evident in Christian or other religious history).

_____

_____

Cyclic time could refer to natural seasons, to a macro-economic business cycle of boom and bust, or the yuga cycle from Hindu cosmology in which each period lasts for over four million years. More recently, we have become aware of the El Niño/La Niña cycles, and anticipate weather phenomenon accordingly.

_____

_____

Progressive time was the aspect of time favoured by the Whig view of history as a series of events during which human life experience and life chances became better, as measured by the desires and ideals of mainly western capitalist democracies. The development of a technological, rationalist, secular mentality was characterized as 'growth', and the reverse was 'regressive'.

_____

_____

Degenerative time is familiar from the 'decline and decadence' narratives favoured by historians who perceived their society in terminal decline, as well as historians who have written during periods of extreme human duress such as the Black Death, and the Cold War.

_____

_____

Related concepts include philosophical ideas such as **Bergsonian Duration, Longtermism and Deep Time**, which refer to wider or deeper ways of perceiving time. They are important in one way or another to the way historians have delineated *what* they will write about, and *how* it has been experienced by the humans they study. Some historians, particularly those of the Annales school, have insisted on an interplay of different aspects of time.

As we have become more secular, multi-cultural, and technologically sophisticated, our concept of time has become more elastic. Chinese and Islamic calendars are not the same as the Gregorian calendar. Similarly, very big scales of time (the cosmological decade, a division of the lifetime of the cosmos) and very small (the 'shake' or 10 nanosecond unit which is used to time events during a nuclear explosion) have become part of human activity and endeavour. They must be taken into account because they inform the way that some humans think, reckon, and act.

Samples from Crawford Lake in Canada may provide the 'golden spike' needed to confirm a new geological epoch – the Anthropocene.

Time is also an important concept because our habit of using an event (the birth of Jesus, the Hijira, the colonization of the Americas, the Atom Bomb) as a demarcation point *from which* or *before which* to begin our study is deeply ingrained in the discipline. History is generally accepted as beginning with the invention of writing. Events before this are considered 'prehistory'. This reminds us of an important assumption: that history is the study of what humans have done, and that humans are the principal agents of the events that we experience.

Yet our alteration of the planet's climate has made it a powerful and present actor in our timescale. What had been the longest or slowest-changing layer of Fernand Braudel's schema is becoming the middle or even top layer. Our own actions have brought the environment into our history with such immediacy that some historians have suggested we accept the environment as an equal actor in the human timescale. If we accept the environment as an agent in our history and one of equal interest and importance to humans, we must widen the time-scope occupied by history to include events important to this new player in human life. This involves considering new forms of 'text' and new ways of reading these texts which will bring historians even more closely into contact with other disciplines.

History in the Anthropocene

To an extent, postmodernism has been recognized as an extreme and unacknowledged version of 4-3rd century BC skepticism, which has limited public and intellectual utility and can easily be hijacked by those with *malice prepense*. After 2000, historians faced questions about how history should be written in the face of Islamist terrorism, the rise or resurgence of China, and an accelerating cycle of economic crises exacerbated by pandemics and new hostilities between superpowers. The narrative of uncomplicated progress is largely bankrupt in view of widening global inequalities, but there is no 'end to history' as Fukuyama predicted.

An even larger challenge lies in the global effects of climate change. Some historians argue that we should now be thinking in terms of an Anthropocene Epoch, defined by human activity rather than forces of nature. The word Anthropocene was coined in the 1980s then popularised in 2000 by chemists Paul J. Crutzen and Eugene F. Stoermer who suggested that we are living in a new geological epoch characterised by the power of humans to effect significant change on planetary systems. Other people, however, argue that humanity is an 'event' not an 'epoch', and that we are a blip on the face of 'deep time'.

In the past sixty years, the impact of human activity on the physical, chemical, and biological systems of our planet has accelerated and become more pronounced. However, it is still unclear whether we should actually name a geological epoch after these effects. The International Commission on Stratigraphy determines the naming of epochs, and they are still looking for a 'golden spike' – that is, a human-effected marker in the fossil record which would be detectable in the planet's geology in millions of years. The presence of this spike would demarcate the Holocene from the Anthropocene. Such terms, however, can have different purposes. Even if humanity may have disappeared in 100 million years, the term 'Anthropocene' communicates an important idea: that our species has a completely disproportionate effect. Some scientists and historians have argued that one of the barriers to recognizing this is our immense *hubris*, which historians have cultivated with narratives of human supremacy – narratives which now seem to have promoted a pseudo-progress.

Clarify

9. Do you think that historians have a moral responsibility to rewrite the traditional narrative of 'high points' of human achievement such as the agrarian revolution, Renaissance, and Industrial Revolution, in view of the environmental changes we now recognise that they triggered?

___

The renaming of the post-1945 epoch has implications for the perception of 'historical' time: if we imagine the Anthropocene beginning with the Industrial Revolution, does this mean that we believed events on Earth before that were directed primarily by some force other than the human? Does the recognition that human agency is now the strongest geopolitical force *necessarily* mean that the History written about it must carry a moral element?

Criticism of the separation of human and natural history was made by Vico, Croce, Collingwood and, most recently, Dipesh Chakrabarty. The acceptance of Environmental History as one of the genres of the discipline officially occurred in 2000, although the academy had been building towards it since 1977. In that year the American Society for Environmental History was founded, and their journal *Environmental History* remains the most important in the field. In 2000 the creation of a European society (ESEH) was announced at the International Congress of Historical Sciences in Oslo.

The French historian Gregory Quenet, writing about 'The Anthropocene and the Time of Historians' in *Annales* says that:

> The Anthropocene cannot be accepted as a historical period without losing a considerable degree of complexity in ... the heterogeneity and discontinuities that constitute human societies, which are inscribed in a plurality of spaces and temporalities, and which produce their contexts instead of fitting into a preexisting condition. However, this debate emphasizes the absolute need to enrich the thresholds of history (up to now too exclusively human), to historicize exchanges with materials (too often considered inert), and to redefine the notion of collectives (still attached to a dated figure of emancipation). ... it is more important than ever to show the strength of the analytical tools of the history of collective relations with nature, and not to let the past become a simple reservoir of progressively illegible examples.

Studying these 'collective relations' is the stated purpose of David Christian's *Maps of Time* (2004) and its accompanying 'Big History' project at Macquarie University in Australia. In the same year the *Encyclopaedia of World Environmental History* appeared, which united two new influences: environmental and global history. While Big History drew in new types of literacy (scientific), and interdisciplinary conversations between historians and scientists, environmental history has involved engagement with political science. As Fernando Sanchez-Marcos has pointed out:

> Environmental history can take different approaches, according to the philosophical anthropology on which they rely. It can be approached from the conviction that the fundamental point of reference is the human being — not as the absolute owner of nature, but as a user of it for his benefit. With this approach there is no opposition, although there is moderate prevention, of "anthropic action" (human intervention) in nature.
>
> Another possible approach to environmental history is the radically geocentric one, according to which Gaia (the Earth) has total priority over human beings. This perspective demands the preservation of a natural environment transformed into a living whole and the supreme value.

Yet the Big History project reminds us that the view of historical and pre-historical time hinges on the presence of literacy, one of the most politicised concepts in the set which social historians can study. Some historians now consider that we should extend our understanding of historical time to include pre-literate periods and point out that the unwillingness to do this has been the result of a restrictive set of cultural assumptions which must, for our own survival, be dispensed with. Daniel Smail has argued that excluding these pre-literate humans really reflects a religious perspective which seeks to deny that 'humans are part of nature, and that human systems are natural systems.' What Smail calls Deep History will focus on 'trends and processes more than events and persons,' requiring historians to read more into archaeological, DNA, and geological data.

The use of DNA-derived evidence has revolutionized our ability to answer legal and historical questions, although the answers do not always bring closure to long-standing social myths. (Even the refusal of certain stories to admit defeat in the face of more and scientific evidence reflects the preference for those narratives, perhaps because their 'emplotment' shores up power structures, identities, or other narratives). From the ability to pinpoint where the species came from, to our understanding of the geographical divergence of different strands of *homo sapiens*, DNA can tell its own story. It can also reveal the inaccuracies in other, more recent stories about individuals.

A controversial example of this was the claim that Thomas Jefferson fathered children on Sally Hemings, one of his slaves at Monticello. Most historians denied rumours that President Jefferson had such a relationship, saying that one of his nephews had been the father of Hemings' children. After genetic evidence confirmed that Jefferson had fathered at least one of Hemings' children, the received story had to be entirely reimagined. Annette Gordon-Reed's *Thomas Jefferson and Sally Hemings: An American Controversy*, for example, reconstructs Jefferson's relations with slaves and slavery. Historian John

Hope Franklin said that

> These things [interracial liaisons] were part of the natural landscape in Virginia, and Mr. Jefferson was as likely as any others to have done this because it's in character with the times—and indeed, with him, who believed in exploiting these people that he controlled completely.

Slavery and the histories of enslaved persons reflects a further trend in recent historiography: that of global history, which focuses on connections and comparisons between societies that have come into contact with each other through 'encounters'. The resulting changes – to environmental and biological aspects, for examples – yoke together other new developments in historiography. As a consequence, despite the post-modern aversion to its grandiose claims and habit of generalization, the grand narrative has made a comeback. C.A. Bayly's *The Birth of the Modern World 1780-1914* (2004) argues that grand narratives are the only way to corral so much data into a sensible narrative which readers will understand. This does not mean that the narrative must be a sweeping one throughout: Timothy Brook's *Vermeer's Hat* (2008) is a microhistory of the objects in Vermeer's paintings, which he adduces as evidence of a 'global' economic community in the seventeenth century. Global history has even impacted historiography – Daniel Woolf's *A Global History of History* (2011) puts the Greco-Roman foundations of western history – writing in the context of other traditions. This, it has been suggested, is one way to even up the disparity with which historiographical writing in non-western societies is viewed. Natalie Zemon Davis has suggested that

> If a new decentered global history is discovering important alternate historical paths and trajectories, then it might also do well to let its big stories be alternated or multiple. The challenge for global history is to place these narratives creatively within an interactive frame.

Transnational history challenges the hegemony of national frameworks, stressing the interaction between events in two or more countries (e.g. dictatorship in the period 1919-1939 studied in the HSC Core). 'Special relationships' such as that between the UK and USA, or China and Australia, can show how nations construct themselves on the basis of a transnational relationship. Transnational history can also vindicate the role that non-Western societies have played in world history, as Jerry Bentley and Herbert Ziegler argued in *Tradition and Encounters: A Global Perspective on the Past* (2000), which does not take any specific civilization as its centre-point, but rather focuses on the progressive convergence of different societies. The presence of significant numbers of nationals from one country within another also challenges the exclusivity which seems to define a nation and its boundaries. By examining the nature of boundary states and events, a new way of looking at national and trans-national myths can emerge. Patricia Nelson Limerick has shown that the American West was less of a 'frontier settlement' where white 'pioneers' faced off against hostile or oppressed native Americans, and more of a melting-pot, 'one of the great meeting zones of the planet' where European, Hispanic, Native American, African-Americans and Asians came together to create a new society.

In 1988 the American historian Peter Novick wrote that 'as a broad community of discourse, as a community of scholars united by common aims, common standards and common purposes, the discipline of history has ceased to exist.' Judged purely by numbers of students taking the subject at secondary and tertiary levels of study, this is clearly untrue, and even the fact that there was a market for a published statement like this shows the paradox of postmodern pessimism about History's survival. History, as an articulation of our need to understand who we are and how we stand in the stream of time, can adapt to the changing circumstances of both authors and readers while adhering to principles of truth and accuracy. In this process, historiography, history's critical self-reflection, has established itself as history's life insurance policy.

Clarify

10. Do you think that 'Global History' is really a new development, or simply the 'same old History' with unparalleled access to sources? Is it a qualitatively new history or just the culmination of what History was always driving towards? Justify your answer.

Think laterally

11. Given the type of knowledge needed to achieve Global History, the resources which fuel it will always come from developed nations. What effect do you think such History writing will have on the concerns of those further down the hegemony?

Reading task 9

Read the following extract from a now-famous article by Gertrude Himmelfarb, 'A neo-luddite on the internet', first published in *The Chronicle for Higher Education*, 1st November 1996.

The intellectual revolution of our time, post-modernism, long antedated the internet. None the less, the internet reinforces post-modernism: it is as subversive of "linear," "logocentric," "essentialist" thinking, as committed to the "aporea," [*i.e. the difficulty of establishing the truth or falsity of something because there is evidence for both*] objections to "indeterminacy," "fluidity," "intertextuality" and "contextuality" of discourse, as deconstruction itself. Like post-modernism, the internet does not distinguish between the true and the false, the important and the trivial, the enduring and the ephemeral. The search for a name or phrase or subject will produce a comic strip or advertising slogan as readily as a quotation from the Bible or Shakespeare. Every source appearing on the screen has the same weight and credibility as every other; no authority is "privileged" over any other.

1. Himmelfarb argues that the internet 'flattens' intellectual privilege by making all sources equal; Ranke insisted on source-based history, and Carr argued that the historian selects some sources and not others. What effect does this flattening have on source-based history and the selection of sources?

2. Himmelfarb contrasts the retrieval and recombination of material with understanding. What do you think she means by 'understanding' written material?

3. Read again Himmelfarb's description of the two forms of thinking: 'essentialist' and 'post-modernist.' Give an example of a time before 1900 when features of 'post-modernism' (aporea, intertextuality, fluidity etc) were evident in historiographical thinking.

4. Himmelfarb's argument against the internet rests primarily on the tool's inability to evaluate or establish hierarchies of authority for the information it contains. Is this a helpful way to think about the historian's tools? Explain your reasons.

ISBN 9780645591422

5. The entire article is only available to subscribers of *The Chronicle of Higher Education* – not even JSTOR has a copy. An edited version of it is available in the right-wing magazine *Prospect* at https://www.prospectmagazine.co.uk/magazine/aneoludditeontheinternet

How does the subscription-only aspect of the article's original publisher reflect on Himmelfarb's own politics? Does this make her argument more or less persuasive?

_____

_____

_____

_____

_____

_____

_____

_____

_____

_____

_____

6. Read 'The Promises and Perils of Digital History', by Daniel J. Cohen and Roy Rosenzweig. It is hosted by the Roy Rosenzweig Center for History and New Media, at George Mason University in Virginia. Summarize the argument it makes in response to Himmelfarb. http://chnm.gmu.edu/digitalhistory/introduction/

_____

_____

_____

_____

_____

_____

_____

_____

7. Consider the different sponsors of the two articles you have read: one was a commercial publication, *The Chronicle for Higher Education*, and the other was a privately-funded project at a university. Do you think it is important that the reader is aware of the provenance of these articles?

_____

_____

Chapter revision statement

Write a list of the key points from this chapter.

_____
_____
_____
_____
_____
_____
_____
_____
_____

Use the list to write a short statement about important features in the discipline of History during the period studied in this chapter.

_____
_____
_____
_____
_____
_____
_____

Notes

_____
_____
_____
_____
_____
_____
_____
_____

Chapter 10: The Student Historiographer

In practical terms, your understanding of this topic will be tested in two places:

1. The Section 1 question in the Trial and HSC exam

2. The historical investigation about 'an area of changing historical interpretation'.

Think of the historiography topic as a tool-kit that helps you to identify where historians in the Case Study are coming from, what thinking has shaped their view, and how the whole debate can be mapped. If you are doing subjects like Extension English, Economics, Society and Culture, or even Senior Science, you'll notice the same historical trends in thought and method there too.

The Section I Essay

It's tempting to memorize an answer but not advisable. The questions for Section 1 cover a wide variety of historical issues. You can't know what will be asked or what the sources will be given. The questions listed on p.1 of this workbook outline what you should know. Go over answers to them in your own mind, decide what you think about them, and what you know most about. You'll be assessed on:

- Demonstration of knowledge and understanding of **relevant** issues of historiography
- Use of **relevant** sources to support your argument
- Creation of a comprehensive, **logical** and sustained response.

Relevant is the key word here: the Section I essay should not be an attempt to tell 'the story of History', beginning with Herodotus and ending with the Anthropocene movement.

This means that **you must have ideas and opinions.** As you read back through this workbook for revision, you should consider:

1. With whom you agree and disagree, and why
2. What does this tell you about your intrinsic attitude to the discipline of History?
3. What influences in school and in your life have made you think this way?
4. What alternative ways of thinking are there – and why have you rejected them?

Remember also that you do not need to agree entirely with one thinker: 'to an extent' is a judicious phrase. Even more judicious is saying exactly where and why you stop agreeing with them.

In the exam

A sensible way to approach the essay is to read the whole question and the sources without leaping to conclusions. <u>Do not try to answer it immediately</u>. Then:

1. **Paraphrase** When you've read the sources carefully paraphrase what they're actually saying. Try to boil it down to a sentence.
2. **Answer contingently** What's your gut reaction to the question?
3. **Look for support** Do your sources agree or disagree with you?
4. **Look more widely** What other authors have relevant ideas about this?
5. **Answer argumentatively** Now plan your argument.

An example

Here is an example from the 2019 HSC History Extension paper. The question was:

To what extent does historical evidence shape the construction of history?

For reasons of copyright the sources cannot be printed – which is in itself an indication of the market forces at work in education.

Source A was from Norman J. Wilson's *History in Crisis? Recent Directions in Historiography* (2005). Wilson said that historians 'never seem to write the book they set out to write' because they are always going through a 'process of dialectical feedback in which evidence and hypothesis constantly modify each other.' He defined history as a 'continual, open-ended process of argument' and said that no answer was final, only good, coherent arguments.

Source B was from Giselle Byrnes' 2012 *The Myths We Live By: Reframing History for the 21st Century* in which she said that 'stories of the past are always changing: that is, our present-day values and attitudes inform how we look back and review what has gone before. Moreover, the questions we put to the past are invariably shaped by our present. 'History' is, therefore, a constant conversation with the past.' She also noted that most historians rejected the idea that that there is an absolute standard of objectivity – the quest for objectivity is, she said, 'like nailing jelly to the wall'. It is impossible to recreate the 'totality of the past' because we're limited by what remains, and this determines whether some stories are told and others silenced. The reasons for that, she claimed, were a preoccupation of her generation of historians.

One way to approach this question was:

1. **Paraphrase each source**

(Source A) Modifying hypotheses according to evidence is simply good empirical method, but it also means that there's no end to History because either the evidence changes or historians do.

(Source B) Societies change the way they think, so we're always going back over the past and looking for things that previous historians missed or ignored.

2. **Answer contingently** My gut reaction is: 'entirely – evidence always shapes the way history is written.' But after an attempt to define the terms helps here – it's not always true.

3. **Look for support** Source A paints a picture of a conscientious historian who carefully revises his argument when the evidence doesn't support. But lots of historians don't do this. They fudge evidence or 'write around' problematic evidence because their hypothesis is fun, or controversial, or popular.

Source B reminds us of changing ideas and beliefs – what, for example, counts as evidence? Historians haven't always agreed about this. Further, the *way* history is constructed often has more to do with the style and interests of the time than what the evidence actually supports.

The evidence only has perhaps *half* the responsibility for the shape of History's construction (Source A). The rest is down to contextual values, style, and interpersonal or interdisciplinary argument (Source B).

3. **Look more widely** Historians who have discussed problems of evidence or the dialectical method include Ibn Khaldun, Valla, Vico, Dilthey, Croce and Ladurie. Historians who have discussed the impacts of personality, style, and contextual values include Polybius, Eusebius, Gibbon, Geertz, White, Chakrabarty, and the 'telly-dons'. Clearly, to bring in all of these would be impossible in the time available, but I can confidently make references to their ideas and link them to the sources in the question.

4. **Answer argumentatively**

To what extent does historical evidence shape the construction of history?

Thesis: *To a moderate extent: partly evidence but also style, personality, and values*

The construction of history is only partly shaped by evidence. Literary style, contextual values, and the impossibility of closure are also vitally influential.

Point 1 *Evidence – what counts, how, types of knowledge*

Evidence does indeed shape history by provoking questions from which we form hypotheses. But what counts as evidence has changed, and our understanding of *how* we find evidence, has also grown over time.

Point 2 *Contextual values*

Historical questions reflect changing values, which has become more rational, secular and global – in the West. Historians themselves are products of their time and also reflect its the values.

Point 3 *Style and closure*

A historian's audience also affects the construction of their work. The character of history as an ongoing argument means that it will likely never end.

At that point, you are ready to attempt the answer. The sample essay which follows is longer than an exam essay, but you should think of it as a formative piece of writing – an important exercise for the exam itself.

To what extent does historical evidence shape the construction of history?

At first glance it seems that evidence shapes the construction of history to a significant and unique extent. Most modern historians distinguish history from fiction because historical activity is constrained by what evidence there is and how much it supports the inferences drawn - this underpins Norman Wilson's rather idealistic description of modern historical method. Yet historians have not always agreed on what counts as evidence or what kind of narrative may be drawn from it. As Giselle Byrnes notes, contextual values governing the questions we put to that evidence, and even what we regard as worthy of historical interest, shape the construction of history just as much as the texts and artefacts left over from the past. Literary style, also, and histories' participation in broader debates which preclude closure, suggest that evidence is in fact only one factor shaping the construction of history.

The concept of evidence - sources' support for a narrative hypothesis - has characterised historical endeavour since Herodotus. Intrinsic to his method was the acknowledgement and evaluation of that evidence: he foregrounded the fact that the claims and questions which constituted his narrative were informed by sources of differing evidential weight. The conscious presence of evidence as evidence is apparent in historians as varied as Bede, Hume, von Ranke, and historians of the digital age who embed hyperlinks to evidence just as Eusebius copied into his work documents otherwise inaccessible to the reader. The presence of the claim, the evidence, and the evaluation of the evidence results in the three-dimensional writing that we recognize as history as distinguished from fiction, which is under no obligation to provide evaluated external evidence for the claims it makes. Indeed, the fact that new ways of thinking about evidence produce new histories supports the idea that the construction of history is shaped by the evidence.

Yet what counts as evidence has not always been agreed upon by historians; pre-twentieth century historians' refusal to engage with 'unofficial' sources such as the products of women, slaves, and outsiders, reflects evidence's contentiousness as a concept. Early historians preferred textual evidence perhaps because of physical limitations which made access to items, places and people difficult, but it was not until the Renaissance that those texts' nature and veracity were systematically interrogated. Lorenzo Valla's demonstration of the Donation of Constantine as an early-medieval forgery and Jean Mabillon's development of diplomatic, inform any attempt to gauge how much history's construction is shaped by evidence in two ways. For one thing, Valla's and Mabillon's works show how much pre-Renaissance historians worked around the evident limitations of some textual evidence – limitations which a conservative historical tradition preferred to ignore (since many, particularly ecclesiastical historians continued to use the Donation as evidence of an unbroken continuity from antiquity to contemporaneity). This indicates how much more authoritative underlying belief paradigms can be than the picture of good historical method Norman Wilson paints. In some notorious examples like the Hitler diaries, evidence is produced to fit a favoured hypothesis, not vice versa, as Wilson has it. Secondly, the uses to which these discredited sources are put shows that the relationship of hypothesis to evidence is not really linear but symbiotic. The 'discredited' item is ripe to provide evidence of something else, but of what exactly depends in part on the values which inform our questions. The mid-20th century history of 'mentalities' *a la* Robert Mandrou, or the revelation from DNA evidence that Thomas Jefferson was indeed the father of some of Sally Hemmings' children are examples of the symbiotic (rather than sequential) relationship between evidence and historical enquiry. Certainly, evidence is central to the shape of historical activity, but however often it is resifted, several other factors contribute almost as much to the construction of history.

The questions that we put to this evidence come from the values which shape the historian. The 'conversation' to which Wilson and Byrnes allude is a conversation between present values and real or perceived values from the past. That contextual values predispose historians to some evidence is apparent in Herodotus, who included information about women and foreigners because his values (compared to Thucydides' elite male politico-military values) acknowledged their place within the wider cultural and social world which brought about Persian failure. Even when the evidence used is largely the same, different values result in different constructions, as a comparison of histories of the English Civil War show. The most vivid example of how contextual values shape history's construction is in literary style: *how* each age tells a story and prefers to read (or view) one has just as great an influence on the construction of history as the evidence which backs that story up. As Robert Rosenstone has noted, for example, documentaries can analyse textual evidence much more easily than can docu-dramas. This does not mean, as Hayden White claimed, that history is no more than style or 'emplotment', but for stories which depart from the traditional repertoire of plots, or have antagonists from the same culture and institutions as the historian, new types of evidence must be found. Subaltern studies, for example, interrogates the silences of colonialism (as Byrnes notes), and questions how historians can 'recover' evidence for something that was never really regarded as a thing in its own right. Again, evidence of our values changing with respect to the physical environment is apparent in ecohistory and the 21st century Anthropocene movement, which foreground the literal background, juxtaposing human agency with the voiceless terrain, and measuring their interactions. The values which precede historical hypotheses are thus just as important to history's construction as the evidence used to support it.

Those values also inform historians' awareness of their audience. Elite male readers and writers have, historically, accounted for history's politico-military focus, its treatment of 'great men' and densely-written character. Academic historians write for each other, producing the heavily referenced *mis-en-page* of academic history which reflects the ongoing conversation to which both Wilson and Byrnes refer. Regardless of what historians like Keith Jenkins suggest about 'simply waving goodbye to history' this conversation also precludes closure or finality. Indeed, the historical debate itself can become the subject of historical writing, as th perennial interest in 'Causes of the First World War' shows. The digital world – now historicized in its own right, even by neo-Luddites like Gertrude Himmelfarb who use the internet to excoriate it – has also spawned 'citizen historians' who contribute to and control historical activity in free and open-source sites. Popular historians' desire for sales, citizens' desire to control the record of their historical existence, and academic historians' desire for the last word all shape the histories they construct. That most histories position themselves in relation to an existing debate greatly influences the shape that they take; the presence of this unending argument is at least as important to the construction of history as the evidence on which it calls.

Evidence is characteristic of historical writing; it shapes histories' construction to a significant, but not unique, extent. Equally powerful are our assumptions about what constitutes a historical matter, about the mechanics of proof, about what people want to read and how, about our academic antagonists and how they will respond. All of these shape the construction of history, which is by nature as variable and as is Byrnes' 'jelly nailed to a wall.'

The historical investigation

The historical investigation must deal with *significant historical questions* and *an area of changing historical interpretation*.

You can think of this as a three-step process:

1. The significant question
2. The historical concepts involved
3. A debate which exemplifies perspectives on the question

Significant historical questions include:

Each question involves the concepts covered by the **Concept Focus** pages. All the questions have been taken up by the people and debates described in this workbook.

ISBN 9780645591422

To choose the topic of your historical investigation

1. Go back through this workbook and note any ideas, people, or debates which have interested you.

2. Outline the historical questions they have deal with. You can use the graphic to help you.

3. If you don't already know what debate or changing interpretation was involved, look it up. The Institute of Historical Research (https://www.history.ac.uk/) is a good place to start. You can follow two paths on their website:

   a. Special Issue reviews on a particular topic or debate
      https://www.history.ac.uk/publications/reviews-history

   b. Archives, resources, and articles
      https://archives.history.ac.uk/makinghistory/resources/articles/

When you have read a bit about the area of historical writing you should be able to identify one question which has arisen in it, and who the participants in that debate have been. From there you should research their positions, and resolve your own perspective on it.

An example

1. Noting areas of interest

   i. Environmental history
   ii. The 'decadence' / 'decline and fall' grand narrative
   iii. Hayden White's 'emplotment' of historical writing

2. Identifying the significant question and the concepts involved

   i. *Environmental history: What is history – especially, what's its scope?*
      Concepts: historical consciousness; grand narratives; auxiliary sciences; the public; time

   ii. *The decadence/decline and fall narratives: Why do we do history? Who does history?*
       Concepts: grand narratives; style; nationalist history; debate; the historian themselves

   iii. *Hayden White's 'emplotment' of historical writing: How is history done? What are its components?*
        Concepts: grand narratives; style; the public

3. Finding an example of a debate about the question (choose ONE from the list above, and research it until you decide to dispense with that area).

Environmental history. Reading the Institute of Historical Research's article on *environmental history* I noticed that British, European, and American historians were discussed but not Australian ones.

So I looked up 'Australian Environmental History' and found out that, since 2009, there has been a Centre for Environmental History at the ANU. There is a reasonably long bibliography for Australian Environmental History at https://www.eh-resources.org/bibliography-australian-environmental-history/, much of it published since 2000.

However, I also found an article (https://insidestory.org.au/tearing-down-and-building-up/) which said that in 1981, 'Geoffrey Bolton wrote what we might consider to be Australia's first national synthesis of environmental history', a book called *Spoils and Spoilers*. This article also gave a very thorough biography of Bolton. It also alluded to several areas of debate, and questions about:

- how environmental history should be conducted,
- what it really covered,
- what its relationships were with other historical areas such as economic history, social and material history, and nationalist history.

I discovered that Bolton's book had appeared at a time when Australia was engaged in a celebration of its nationhood (the bicentennial celebrations of 1988), and wondered how his story of despoliation and agrarian disaster was received by historians and a public celebrating a nation built on resource-exploitation and agrarian success.

At this point, I decided that there was enough interesting material to write my historical investigation about environmental history, and used JSTOR to develop a short reading list of five articles to start with:

JSTOR search: Geoffrey Bolton AND 'spoils and spoilers'

Returned: 49 results

Selection:

1. McNeill, J. R. "Observations on the Nature and Culture of Environmental History." *History and Theory*, vol. 42, no. 4, 2003, pp. 5–43. *JSTOR*, http://www.jstor.org/stable/3590677. Accessed 9 Aug. 2023.

2. FROST, WARWICK. "Australia Unlimited? Environmental Debate in the Age of Catastrophe, 1910-1939." *Environment and History*, vol. 10, no. 3, 2004, pp. 285–303. *JSTOR*, http://www.jstor.org/stable/20723494. Accessed 9 Aug. 2023.

3. Killingray, David. *Teaching History*, no. 34, 1982, pp. 43–43. *JSTOR*, http://www.jstor.org/stable/43254495. Accessed 9 Aug. 2023.

4. ROBIN, LIBBY, and TOM GRIFFITHS. "Environmental History in Australasia." *Environment and History*, vol. 10, no. 4, 2004, pp. 439–74. *JSTOR*, http://www.jstor.org/stable/20723505. Accessed 9 Aug. 2023.

5. Capps, Maura. "Fleets of Fodder: The Ecological Orchestration of Agrarian Improvement in New South Wales and the Cape of Good Hope, 1780–1830." *Journal of British Studies*, vol. 56, no. 3, 2017, pp. 532–56. *JSTOR*, https://www.jstor.org/stable/26599096. Accessed 9 Aug. 2023.

ISBN 9780645591422

Preparing your investigation

List the areas of interest. Choose no more than THREE.

___

Look at the graphic on p.173. What historical questions and concepts are involved in these areas?

___

Begin with the first area of interest. Look it up in history.ac.uk or another guide which will provide you with more information.

What debates, publications, and people are important in this area?

ISBN 9780645591422

Chapter revision statement

Write a list of the key points from this chapter.

_____
_____
_____
_____
_____
_____
_____
_____
_____
_____

Use the list to write a short statement about important features in the discipline of History during the period studied in this chapter.

_____
_____
_____
_____
_____
_____
_____
_____

Notes

_____
_____
_____
_____
_____
_____
_____

ISBN 9780645591422

ISBN 9780645591422

www.ingramcontent.com/pod-product-compliance
Lightning Source LLC
Chambersburg PA
CBHW081418300426
44109CB00019BA/2339